CHOOSE YOUR ATTITUDE, CHANGE YOUR LIFE

DEBORAH SMITH PEGUES

HARVEST HOUSE PUBLISHERS
EUGENE, OREGON

Cover design by Koechel Peterson & Associates, Inc., Minneapolis, Minnesota

Previously published under the title *30 Days to a Great Attitude*
CHOOSE YOUR ATTITUDE, CHANGE YOUR LIFE
Copyright © 2009 by Deborah Smith Pegues
Published by Harvest House Publishers
Eugene, Oregon 97408
www.harvesthousepublishers.com

Library of Congress Cataloging-in-Publication Data
   Pegues, Deborah Smith, 1950-
   [30 days to a great attitude]
   Choose your attitude, change your life / Deborah Smith Pegues.
      pages cm
   Includes bibliographical references.
   ISBN 978-0-7369-5827-1 (pbk.)
   ISBN 978-0-7369-5828-8 (eBook)
   1. Attitude change—Religious aspects—Christianity. 2. Conduct of life.
   I. Title.
   BV4597.2.P44 2014
   248.4—dc23

                           2013015779

Printed in the United States of America

19 20 21 22 23 / BP-JH / 10 9 8 7 6 5

*This book is dedicated to every reader
who would dare commit to displaying the right
attitude in every situation.*

Acknowledgments

Special thanks to all my friends—including cyber friends—who not only prayed for this project but also willingly shared their experiences and insights on the various attitudes discussed in this book.

I appreciate my entire Harvest House family for their flexibility and commitment to a quality product. Thanks especially to Bob Hawkins Jr., president, and Terry Glaspey, director of acquisitions, for always pushing me to the next level despite my protests. My editor, Rod Morris, is always a refreshing fount of wisdom as he hawks the spiritual integrity of all my biblical conclusions and assertions.

Finally, I'm eternally grateful to my husband, Darnell, for his unselfish support, his willingness to sacrifice our time together, and for being the most loving and self-sufficient husband in the world.

Contents

Prologue:

Commit to Change

"Alice, I understand you were suspended from school today. What happened?" Ann quizzed her niece.

"My teacher disrespected me, and when people disrespect me, that's what they're going to get back from me," Alice said.

Although only eleven years old, Alice's attitude was already entrenched. How had she developed such a mindset? Ann knew that Alice was merely repeating her grandmother's mantra: "People who don't respect you don't deserve your respect."

Yes, our attitude programming starts early in life. We often learn the most destructive ones from our parents, grandparents, or other authority figures we trust implicitly but who often see themselves as victims of life's inequities. Unfortunately, Granny failed to tell Alice that such an attitude would sabotage her relationship with her teachers, other people, and her career even though it seemed eons away. Besides her grandmother, Alice's attitude will be shaped by how others respond to her, her friends, the books she reads, her job, and several other factors. Every single day she will have to decide how to frame and respond to the inevitable negative experiences of life.

That's what this book is about. It is not a pep talk on maintaining a positive attitude. Volumes of good books have already been written on that. I will not subject you to another "think positively" general approach to the subject. Rather, I will explore 30 specific attitudes that can make or break our personal and professional relationships. For each one discussed, I will provide practical guidelines on how you can integrate it into your daily interactions. If you need a more exhaustive treatment of a particular attitude, be proactive and search the Internet and your local library for other resources.

In this book, you will meet modern-day and biblical examples of people who did or did not model the right attitude in their responses to given situations. From intolerance to an attitude of entitlement to a controlling attitude, I will show you how to conquer them all using Scripture-based principles, thought-provoking questions, healing prayers and affirmations, and practical strategies to put into action immediately. While the strategies are simple and doable, they may not always be easy. I will be painfully transparent as I share the various wrong attitudes that challenge me even to this day—despite the fact that I have had good spiritual leaders and mentors and have invested many years in Bible study learning God's way of living life to the fullest.

Yes, like me, you may know the way to victory. Unfortunately knowledge is not the single key to success. We have to commit to change—beginning with a change in our thinking and the emotions that we choose to attach to our thoughts about the inevitable negative situations we encounter. Dr. Caroline Leaf, author and learning specialist, summed it up this way: "Behavior starts with a thought. Thoughts stimulate emotions which then result in attitude and finally produce behavior. This symphony of electrochemical reactions in the body affects the way we think and feel physically. Therefore, toxic thoughts produce toxic emotions, which produce toxic attitudes, resulting in toxic behaviors."[1] Thoughts. Emotions. Attitude. Behavior. Yes, we can control every step of the process.

I finally understand that my attitude determines whether I will be mediocre or excellent, anxious or calm, intolerant or accepting, or whether I exhibit a host of other mindsets that will affect the quality of my life. Since the choice is mine, I've decided to choose wholeness in every aspect of my life—relationally, emotionally, financially, physically, and spiritually.

I invite you to join me on my attitude journey. My hope is that we will learn to display the right attitude in every situation and to be the shining light that dispels the darkness in a negative world.

Day 1

Choose to Connect

Each of us comes into this world alone and we will leave alone. However, God never intended for any man to become an island unto himself. Shortly after He created Adam, God acknowledged that His work was not yet complete. "And the LORD God said, 'It is not good that man should be alone; I will make him a helper comparable to him'" (Genesis 2:18). So, He created Eve. While some like to cite this passage to convince single men to get married, the reality is that regardless of our gender or marital status, we were all created to be in meaningful relationships with other people. If you study the life of Jesus, you will find that He was very sociable and often attended weddings, dinners, and other social events.

The phrase "one another" appears 142 times in the New King James Version. It is clearly God's divine plan that we connect and communicate with other people in a mutually beneficial, satisfying, and productive way. To behave otherwise is counter to God's purpose for His creation. And it is our responsibility to take the initiative in connecting with others. "A man who has friends must himself be friendly" (Proverbs 18:24).

To be aloof or emotionally detached is detrimental not only to your personal life but also to your career or business. In some professions, an aloof attitude can spell the death of a relationship. Have you ever been to a doctor or other medical service provider who treated you with cold indifference? Were you eager to see him again? What judgments did you make about him?

And what about emotionally distant people who provide other services? I was shopping at a store recently and the clerk was very aloof despite my attempts to draw her out with small talk. Knowing there were other vendors in the area who sold similar products, I silently vowed to strike that store off my list for future shopping. Rest assured, when you are aloof, people are likely making judgments about you.

Now before I get my rope to hang every aloof person I've ever met, I confess that at times I have pretended to be aloof to avoid having people engage me in conversation, such as when I've wanted to read on an airplane. I usually repented and struck up a conversation since the Holy Spirit was quick to convict me for not taking advantage of an opportunity to talk about the Lord and the status of the person's soul.

Perhaps, for reasons that you justify, you have found yourself putting emotional distance between yourself and others. What were you trying to avoid or protect yourself from? What message were you sending that you didn't have the courage to communicate with words?

As with most negative social behavior, aloofness is learned in childhood. An aloof person may have experienced a range of negativity in her family of origin or at the hands of unwise teachers, authority figures, or mean classmates. Such experiences include moving frequently to different schools or cities; abandonment; cold and emotionally detached parents; being bullied, teased, or ridiculed; and other negative interactions. All of these experiences shouted, "Connecting with people is painful!" Nevertheless, God does not want us to write off the human race as "unsafe"; rather He wants us to continue to seek connection with others. Once you begin to open up to safe people, the imbalance in your emotions toward aloofness will begin to shift.

Lest I oversimplify the solution to this problem, let me caution that a strong resolution to change is not enough. You need God's help. Luke 8:27-39 gives an account of a socially and spiritually disconnected man who was possessed with many demons. He was homeless, naked, and lived in a cemetery outside the town. Obviously, he did not engage in normal human interactions. But after his encounter with Jesus, who cast the demons out of him, he was ready to connect.

> *Now the man from whom the demons had departed begged Him that he might be with Him. But Jesus sent him away, saying, "Return to your own house, and tell what great things God has done for you." And he went*

his way and proclaimed throughout the whole city what
great things Jesus had done for him (LUKE 8:38-39).

I am not saying that aloofness comes from the influence of an evil spirit; rather it is an emotional handicap
that can be healed by our Lord.

Once you've sought God's help, put your faith in
action by joining a small study group at your church or
a support group. If you have been out of the social loop
at your job, why not ask a few coworkers if you may
join them as they head for lunch? Do you really think
they'll say no? Listen to and chime in on various discussions. Share your knowledge and don't think that you
have to agree with everybody's opinion to be accepted.
Have the courage to say, "I have another perspective."
Even if you have nothing to contribute, ask questions
that show your interest. Resist the spirit of fear when it
tells you to retreat into your shell or to avoid the intimacy of a small setting.

Stay the course. God wants you connected.

Prayer

Father, help me to show myself friendly and to find
safe people to interact with regularly so that I may give
and receive the benefits of relating to those You have
ordained to be in my life. In the name of Jesus, I pray.
Amen.

Day 2

Choose to Let Go of Anger

My friend Arbra Ezell, a Spirit-filled family counselor, passed away in 2008, but her words will live long in my memory, "Anger is a secondary emotion; you must identify the primary emotion that gave rise to it." These primary emotions are our internal responses we assign to external events. They include hurt, humiliation, disappointment, frustration, feeling disrespected, disregarded, overlooked, manipulated, and a host of other complex emotions.

Wouldn't it be great if we would just delay our emotional response to a negative event? For example, suppose several months ago you finalized your plans to celebrate your milestone wedding anniversary with a select group of couples. You've purchased theater tickets for the entire party of eight as an expression of your appreciation of your long-term friendship. The pre-show dinner reservations have been made, and you are looking forward to a great time.

The day before the celebration, Couple X calls and informs you they have friends who are flying in unexpectedly and want to know if they can invite this couple to join the festivities. Of course you haven't read the chapter in this book titled "Choose Flexibility," so you immediately assign the emotion of *annoyance* to what you perceive as a negative event. You and your husband love Couple X dearly, but they have a pattern of making last-minute changes to established plans, which has often frustrated the close-knit group.

What are your choices now? You could advise Couple X that you are trying to create a memory with established friends and do not want the unfamiliar couple to join you, or you could agree to let them come and later display an angry attitude in your impatience with the waitstaff at the restaurant, theater personnel, or even the unfamiliar couple.

This fairly harmless instance demonstrates how easily you can develop an angry attitude. By no means am I minimizing the more serious hurts that many have experienced at the hands of unwise parents, abusive spouses, mean bosses, and others. If you have been hurt in this way and have never brought closure by confronting these issues, you most likely developed an angry attitude toward those who remind you of the original painful event. When others observe this angry attitude, they can often be very judgmental about your behavior and seek to put distance in the relationship without putting forth the least bit of effort to understand your underlying pain.

What good is there in holding on to anger anyway? A wise person once said, "For every minute you're angry, you lose sixty seconds of happiness." An angry attitude thwarts your personal and professional development. Also realize that when you harbor anger, you give whatever or whoever angers you the power over your attitude. It's time to take your power back. God wants you at peace. "Let all bitterness, wrath, anger, clamor, and evil speaking be put away from you, with all malice. And be kind to one another, tenderhearted, forgiving one another, even as God in Christ forgave you" (Ephesians 4:31-32).

The following actions will help you implement your decision to let go of anger:

- Acknowledge the primary hurt or emotion at the root of your anger.

- Become aware of how your anger is manifesting itself (such as surliness or profanity).

- Control anger's impact on your body by inhaling deeply and exhaling with an affirmation such as "Thank You, Father" or "I receive Your peace now."

- Watch your tone and language in all your communications, not just with the person who has angered you. Request rather than demand. You'll feel more in control, and people will be more inspired to cooperate with you.

- Make a decision to forgive. You'll know you have forgiven when you no longer want to see your perpetrator punished. Don't confuse this with the fact that you still feel the hurt. Emotions follow behavior. If you keep reopening the wound by always talking about the offense, it will never heal. Keep doing the right thing. You have a helper, the Holy Spirit.

- Talk to a counselor if you believe you need more hands-on enforcement.

- Avoid vindictive or negative people who encourage your old behavior.

Prayer

Father, help me to put away all wrath and bitterness and to release everybody who has ever hurt me. Show me the opportunity for spiritual and emotional growth in every negative situation. In the name of Jesus, I pray. Amen.

Day 3

Choose to Live Passionately

I heard a story about a high school social studies teacher who, frustrated with the apathy of his students, stormed into the classroom one day and with great indignation wrote A-P-A-T-H-Y on the board in huge letters and placed an exclamation point behind it. He wrote so hard, the chalk broke. Two students, who had been forced to sit in the front row because they had arrived too late for the ever popular seats in the back of the room, looked at him with their normal disinterest. One of them cocked his head to the side and asked his classmate, "What is ah-pay-thigh?" His friend responded, "Who cares?"

Does this sound like your attitude? Are you so focused on your own life that nothing much else matters? Let's look at some factors that may be numbing your compassion, enthusiasm, and motivation.

Lack of Goals. You fall into apathy when your desires stop and you have no target for your energies. What used to excite you? What killed your interest in it? Is it a desire you could rekindle? Go ahead and write down something—anything—that you could start to pursue now. Forget about the potential cost or all the reasons why the idea or activity might not work. Just give your mind the luxury of feeling hopeful and excited about something, even a small thing.

Wrong Goals. Your general lack of motivation could be because you are pursuing a goal imposed upon you by someone else, such as working toward a degree in a subject you hate. Or like Jonah before he was swallowed by the great fish, maybe you are rowing against the tide of God's will for your life. Have you checked in with the Almighty lately to see if this may be so? Did He really lead you to indulge in that luxury item that is now requiring you to work two jobs? Or maybe the time has ended for a goal that was part of God's plan for a certain season of your life. Moving on is sometimes hard, but oh, the joy and peace of knowing you are in the center of His perfect will.

Spiritual Apathy. If your love for God has waned, then it follows that you will not be concerned about the things that concern Him. Bob Pierce, founder of World Vision (a Christian humanitarian organization that fights poverty and injustice for children and their communities around the world), once prayed, "Let my heart be broken by the things that break the heart of God."[2] Loving and caring for our neighbor is among God's top priorities.

Responding to the question, "Who is my neighbor?"

Jesus told a group of Jewish lawyers a parable (Luke 10:25-37) about a Jew on his way to Jericho who was attacked by thieves and left half-dead on the side of the road. A priest came along, saw his plight, and retreated to the other side. A Levite, a priest's helper, came along and responded likewise. Finally, a Samaritan, though a hated outsider, saw the man's condition and showed compassion. He dressed his wounds, took him to a local inn, and paid in advance for a few nights' stay. Jesus proceeded to explain that loving God ought to make us love our neighbor—and our neighbor is anyone who needs us.

But why did the priest and the Levite demonstrate such apathy? We can only surmise they were too focused on their own agenda. Or maybe they were overwhelmed with the magnitude of the problem and didn't want to commit the time and the resources necessary to get the man back on his feet.

I used to feel overwhelmed when I would hear stories of millions of starving children in the world. Then someone convinced me to sponsor one impoverished child in another country. I believe that because of my support, she will impact many. Whatever your reason for doing nothing, it is unacceptable to God. "But whoever has this world's goods, and sees his brother in need, and shuts up his heart from him, how does the love of God abide in him? My little children, let us not love in word or in tongue, but in *deed* and in truth" (1 John 3:17-18, emphasis added). The admonition is simple: "Do something!"

There is nothing more personally rewarding than serving others. Unfortunately, if you have lost your passion for life, you'll be hard-pressed to improve the quality of life for someone else. That's why you must wage an offensive against apathy starting this very moment. For each category below, list one doable goal you believe you can pursue and complete within the next two weeks:

Spiritual goal: _____

(*Example:* Pray 15 minutes as soon as you awaken each day for government, church, family, and other concerns.)

Relational goal: _____

(*Example*: Join Facebook, the online social network, and reconnect with old friends.)

Physical goal: _____

(*Example*: Go for a three-mile walk; ask a few others to join you.)

Professional goal: _____

(*Example*: Become proficient at Microsoft Word by completing the free online tutorial.)

The examples I've given you are all simple activities that can get you moving toward a goal. They require no money, only a commitment to do them. Reignite your passion for life. There are people out there who need what God has deposited in you, and you need what He has deposited in them. It is time to get out of neutral and shift into drive!

Prayer

Father, forgive me for disconnecting from You and becoming apathetic about the many opportunities You have given me to serve. Renew my passion for life and give me compassion for the needs of others. In the name of Jesus, I pray. Amen.

Day 4

Choose to Build Others Up

"So easy, even a caveman can do it!"

GEICO, the American auto insurance company, popularized this phrase with its humorous TV commercials that poke fun at the stupidity of cavemen trying to assimilate into modern culture. It seems that everyone has jumped on the bandwagon and uses it to convey the message, "You're an idiot if you don't get it." While the ads cause us to chuckle, a condescending attitude is no laughing matter; it hurts people. It cuts to the heart of a person's self-esteem, especially if that person tends to be insecure. Of course, most condescending people are battling their own insecurities.

When you behave in a socially or intellectually superior manner to others, it shows lack of respect, grace, and finesse. Most people with a condescending attitude do possess great knowledge and skills; however, they sabotage their success and relationships by their ignorance of basic people skills. I've observed that the downside to being brilliant is that it is often accompanied by impatience with the "slow-thinking moron," which seems to be just about the entire population in the eyes of those blessed with high intelligence and quick wit.

The apostle Paul, being a learned man himself, knew the pitfalls of having an abundance of knowledge and a rich heritage. He cautioned, "For who makes you differ from another? And what do you have that you did not receive? Now if you did indeed receive it, why do you boast as if you had not received it?" (1 Corinthians 4:7). Such a person would do well to realize that his intellect, experience, and exposure are gifts from God. Paul addressed this issue further when he admonished, "Be of the same mind one toward another. Mind not high things, but condescend to men of low estate. Be not wise in your own conceit" (Romans 12:16 KJV). The charge here is to learn how to condescend without being condescending.

Let's look at some commonly used expressions in everyday personal or professional interactions that could be perceived as condescending and how to modify them so that you encourage rather than discourage effective communication.

"Let me make this simple." I have the wonderful privilege as a certified public accountant of serving as the financial consultant to a select number of churches. In presenting the sometimes technical information to their boards of directors or other groups of nontechnically oriented individuals, I have to be on guard against using a phrase such as "let me see if I can make this easy."

Certainly my goal is to make the information as easy to understand as possible, but having studied human behavior for many years, I'm aware that such a statement could be interpreted as "you are intellectually inferior and need mental training wheels to grasp this." A better phrase would be, "Please let me know if I'm not being clear enough on this point."

"That's already on the table." In brainstorming sessions duplicate ideas may be put forth as some people may be so preoccupied with trying to come up with an idea they may not have heard the original suggestion. Don't respond to person X's idea by saying, "We've already thought of that." She could easily interpret that as "You're on the late freight. We're faster thinkers than you." Rather, say, "Thanks, great minds work alike. We're already considering that approach."

"Been there, done that!" When a friend or colleague attempts to share a helpful experience or a suggestion that you've already tried, don't just dismiss it by a curt and impersonal "Been there, done that!" as I see many people do. That's the same as saying "Useless idea!" Simply say, "Thanks for your input."

If you realize after the fact that you made a condescending remark, apologize quickly and explain what your objective was and what you should have said. "I'm sorry, I sounded condescending and I didn't mean to be. I'm really just trying to bring clarity to our discussion and to make sure that we are all on the same page."

Being sensitive to the impact that your condescending remarks can have on another requires prayer and practice.

Once again, the Golden Rule should be your guiding principle. Think how you would feel if someone were to say or do to you what you are about to say or do.

Prayer

Father, I humble myself and acknowledge that everything I know and everything I have are all gifts from You. Teach me to open my mouth with wisdom and to build others up rather than tearing them down. In the name of Jesus, I pray. Amen.

Day 5

Choose to Be Peaceable

"No matter what I say, she always has a 'but' even when we discuss issues neither of us really cares about," George said. "I wonder why she loves arguing so much!"

His exasperation was evident. I knew his wife and silently agreed that she was one contentious woman. A biblical proverb came to mind as I listened to his plight.

> *It is better to dwell in a corner of a housetop,*
> *Than in a house shared with a contentious woman.*
> (PROVERBS 25:24).

Married women, listen up. If your husband has retreated to the "corner of the housetop" emotionally and has virtually stopped communicating, consider whether your attitude drove him there. How easy are you to talk to? Do you really listen to your husband with the intent to understand, or do you make snap judgments about his behavior? Your attitude establishes the fragrance of your home; you choose whether it will be pleasant or whether it stinks.

It has been my joy for over 30 years to create an atmosphere of peace, lightheartedness, acceptance of differences, and honest and direct communication in our home. I make every effort to inspire my husband by affirming and supporting him and his goals. Nagging has not been necessary.

> *A quarrelsome wife is as annoying*
> *as constant dripping on a rainy day.*
> (PROVERBS 27:15 NLT)

Yes, husbands can be contentious too; however, such an attitude is more common among women. And no, I'm not absolving husbands of their responsibility as the spiritual leader of the home to love, protect, and provide for their family. Few things will cause a woman to become more contentious than when he drops the ball in these areas.

Contentiousness is annoying to everybody—except fellow quarrelers. I heard about an amusing bumper sticker that read: "People who think they know it all are especially annoying to those of us who do."

Of course, nagging wives are not the only ones prone to displaying a contentious attitude. It is also prevalent among older people who, fearing uselessness, struggle to prove they still have some level of superior knowledge. Also guilty are the many people of various religious persuasions who contend for their faith, but have not learned to do it in a noncontentious way—even within their own religious group. I've heard stories of people almost coming to blows in a Sunday school class. They have yet to learn that quarreling does not invite change.

What about you? Do you always have to have the last word in a discussion? Do you feel compelled to argue every issue? God's stance on contentiousness is clear: "Don't have anything to do with foolish and stupid arguments, because you know they produce quarrels. And the Lord's servant must not quarrel; instead, he must be kind to everyone, able to teach, not resentful" (2 Timothy 2:23-24 NIV). This passage shows four key strategies for overcoming a contentious attitude.

"Must not quarrel." You really can cut off contention at the pass by simply refusing to engage in a going-nowhere-positive conversation.

> *The beginning of strife is like releasing water;*
> *Therefore stop contention before a quarrel starts.*
> (PROVERBS 17:14)

Why argue with someone who is already set in his beliefs? Calmly plant your seeds of information in a person's mind and commit the issue to God, the only one who can cause a person to be receptive to an idea.

"Be kind to everyone." There is no need to be hostile, condescending, or disagreeable with anybody who does not share your view. What is motivating you toward such unkindness? Must you prove your opponent wrong to validate your self-worth? If the subject matter is not eternal and does not affect the quality of your life, learn to give others the luxury of having their own opinion without your ridicule.

"Able to teach." Be armed with knowledge and capable of presenting it coherently, but don't use it to beat others into submission to your view. Also understand that your ability to teach does not preclude you from being a learner.

"Not resentful." Resentment is nothing more than unresolved anger. Be honest about whatever hurts, disappointments, or disillusionments may be fueling your dogmatic attitude about a particular issue. Ask God for the courage and strength to confront and release it.

Prayer

Father, Your word says that I must not quarrel, so I repent now for every time I have been contentious. I ask that You make me an instrument of peace so that people will be receptive to the truths that You reveal through me. In the name of Jesus, I pray. Amen.

Day 6

Choose to Value
Others' Opinions

Before I began to write each chapter of this book, I examined myself to see if I tend to exhibit the particular attitude before I launched into "fixing" the reader. It took only a few minutes of reflection to realize that I have indeed been dismissive in certain situations. While I'll spare you the details, I will share a couple of the reasons I did so.

In one instance, the target of my dismissive attitude did not have his facts right or attempted to make an argument he could not produce any concrete evidence for. I hate it when people do that (yes, I know, you do too!). I'm determined not to argue with a fool, so I waved him off. In another instance, my target had his facts right, but I had so many stressors at the time that I didn't want to hear about my communication failure, so I dismissed his input to protect myself against the painful truth.

I've seen others adopt a dismissive approach when they have an entrenched attitude toward the issue being discussed or negative feelings about the person making the request or argument. For example, I was walking on the beach with two friends I'll call Rhonda and Sally. Rhonda remarked how much she enjoyed taking in the beauty of the California coastline at sunrise.

"Next time, you should grab your camera and capture the moment," Sally responded.

"Oh please, it's not that serious!"Rhonda said.

I felt bad that Sally's suggestion had been dismissed so insensitively. Of course Sally did have the annoying habit of always telling us what we should be doing. It was still no excuse for how Rhonda responded.

Husbands are often guilty of being dismissive of a wife's concern. This can be a real relationship buster. Consider this conversation between John and Marge when they were returning home from his company's social function.

"Betty seemed to be flirting with you at the party tonight," Marge said.

"Oh, quit being so insecure!" John replied.

John could have said, "Hmmm, I wasn't aware of it. Even so, you're the only one for me." Now how smooth is that? He'd certainly get more mileage out of this response than out of his.

If you are a supervisor or one in authority, you must also be aware of how you respond to the opinions of your subordinates as it can have a detrimental impact on morale and productivity. Even if someone puts forth an idea that you find without merit, you must resist the temptation to dismiss it on the spot. A simple "Thanks for your input" will have a greater impact than "That won't work."

Whatever the relationship, when you are dismissive toward anyone, it sends a message: "Your issue is insignificant to me," "Your feelings or opinions don't matter," "I'm disregarding you or your idea." Spoken or unspoken, these statements cut to the heart of a person's sense of value and need for respect. This is especially true if the person believes he has earned the right to special consideration.

This is demonstrated in the story of Nabal and David in 1 Samuel 25. Nabal was a very rich man who lived in a city some distance from where he sheared his sheep. During David's time of fleeing the wrath of King Saul, he and his 600 men camped near where Nabal's shepherds tended his sheep, providing a wall of protection for them. Later, when they needed food supplies, David sent a contingent to ask Nabal to help them out and to remind him of how they had protected his flock and his shepherds. Nabal responded like the fool that his name meant:

> *Then Nabal answered David's servants, and said, "Who is David, and who is the son of Jesse? There are many servants nowadays who break away each one from his master. Shall I then take my bread and my water and my meat that I have killed for my shearers, and give it to men when I do not know where they are from?"* (1 SAMUEL 25:10-11).

His dismissive attitude almost cost the lives of his

entire household. When David's men told him how Nabal had responded, he ordered them to join him in wiping out everybody and everything associated with Nabal. Had it not been for the intervention of Nabal's beautiful and wise wife, Abigail, all would have been lost. She quickly prepared adequate provisions for the entire army and personally delivered them as a peace offering. She met David en route to destroy Nabal, his family, and workers. David's anger was appeased.

Know that when you are dismissive toward others, many times they will find a way to show their displeasure. You could avoid a relational disaster by becoming more aware of your behavior.

Understand that opinions, needs, and ideas are as personal and individual as taste buds. Just because you don't think a certain way about a matter doesn't mean that you can be dismissive to those who act or think differently. The only solution to this problem is to step outside yourself and listen attentively and purposefully to others and make every effort to fully understand and address their concerns. You'll reap great dividends as a result.

Prayer

Father, forgive me for the insensitivity I have demonstrated in being dismissive to others. With Your help, I commit to listening and responding to others with grace and wisdom. In the name of Jesus, I pray. Amen.

Day 7

Choose to Love Correction

"Sally, you seemed a little harsh with Mary. I think she was embarrassed at being scolded in front of the other teammates."

Gail was struggling to find the right words; she knew how resistant Sally was to feedback. The words were barely out of her mouth before Sally protested.

"Oh no, you don't understand. You see…"

Here we go again, thought Gail. *She always justifies her behavior, no matter how bad it is.* Gail considered herself a close friend, but frankly, she was fed up with Sally's defensive attitude.

Sally stands in sharp contrast to David, the biblical character who rose from shepherd to king of Israel. In instances where he could have justified his ungodly or unwise action, he quickly acknowledged the error of his way. For example, when fleeing the wrath of King Saul, he sought the help of a certain priest—a decision that ultimately caused Saul to order the death of 85 priests and their families. Devastated but not defensive, David told the surviving son of the slain priest who had assisted him, "I have caused the death of all your father's family" (1 Samuel 22:22 NLT). Can you imagine taking full responsibility for such a tragic consequence? In another instance, when the prophet Nathan confronted David about his adultery with Bathsheba and his attempt to cover up her resulting pregnancy by having her husband killed, David simply said, "I have sinned against the LORD" (2 Samuel 12:13).

Would you have the emotional or spiritual maturity to make such an admission? Or do you have a tendency to always defend your actions for fear of being judged, criticized, alienated, or rejected? Do you often feel attacked when someone offers feedback whether it is positive or negative? How do you respond? Do you retreat in silence? Counter-accuse or blame your "attacker"? Make hostile comments? Become sarcastic?

When one is on the defensive—whether in sports, the armed forces, or in day-to-day relationships—he is attempting to protect something from a real or perceived opponent. I have noticed that people who have a low self-evaluation feel they must protect themselves from the criticism and judgments of others. Of course, we are all prone to being defensive from time to time. However, if you find this has become a pattern in your life, you might be wise to implement the recommendations below.

- Listen to yourself and become aware of your tendency to constantly justify your actions.

- Guard against defensive body language. For

example, crossing your arms when someone is offering input could be your subconscious way of saying, "I'm closed to what you're saying." Keep your body language positive (as in looking pleasant while listening intently).

- Counter the anxiety that comes with feeling attacked by breathing deeply and silently praying, "Lord, I receive Your strength now." Combining this physical and spiritual act will help to minimize your emotional response.

- If there is indeed a genuine and credible justification for your action, state it in a calm, unemotional manner. (If you are really brave, ask a trusted friend or coworker if you are being defensive. Then refuse to become defensive if the response is yes.)

- Don't attack your "attacker." Ask her what she would have done in the situation under discussion. Thank her for sharing her insights.

- If you are guilty of a bad decision or wrong behavior, try admitting it long before it comes to the light. A simple, "I made a mistake" will do wonders for your relationships and your confidence once you decide not to let your mistakes define you or sabotage the quality of your life.

- Interject humor into the situation. ("Boy, am I batting a thousand or what?" "Just shoot me!")

- View feedback as a personal growth opportunity and a tool for developing better relationships. Remember, "He who disdains instruction despises his own soul, but he who heeds rebuke gets understanding" (Proverbs 15:32).

Prayer

Father, cause me to love instruction and to resist defensiveness so that I may grow and glorify You in all my interactions. Heal me of my insecurity and my need to be blameless. In the name of Jesus, I pray. Amen.

Day 8

Choose to Value Others

Have you ever alienated someone or deemed her inferior because she did not share or possess an advantage that you enjoyed? Such elitist thinking is not just a modern-day attitude. As far back as the time of Moses, we see this mindset displayed.

When God ordered the Jewish elders to appear before Him for a special anointing during the Israelites' journey to the Promised Land, He poured His Spirit upon all in attendance, and they prophesied. However, two of the elders stayed in the camp and did not attend. Notwithstanding, someone saw them prophesying and quickly reported it to Moses.

> *So Joshua the son of Nun, Moses' assistant, one of his choice men, answered and said, "Moses my lord, forbid them!"*
>
> *Then Moses said to him, "Are you zealous for my*

sake? Oh, that all the LORD's people were prophets and that the LORD would put His Spirit upon them!" (NUMBERS 11:28-29).

Joshua believed only the select group that gathered before the Lord should prophesy. In the New Testament, we find Jesus rebuking His disciples for their elitist attitude:

> *John said to Jesus, "Teacher, we saw someone using your name to cast out demons, but we told him to stop because he wasn't in our group."*
>
> *"Don't stop him!" Jesus said. "No one who performs a miracle in my name will soon be able to speak evil of me. Anyone who is not against us is for us"* (MARK 9:38-40 NLT).

If you are an elitist, you must come to grips with the fact that every advantage or favor you enjoy is a gift from God. Elitism is a form of pride. Humble yourself and realize that what God has given you or allowed you to achieve is for His glory and not your personal exaltation. Even if you think you pulled yourself up by your own bootstraps and achieved your advantage by sheer will and determination, hear the sobering words of the educated and anointed apostle Paul.

> *But whatever I am now, it is all because God poured out his special favor on me—and not without results. For I have worked harder than any of the other apostles; yet it was not I but God who was working through me by his grace* (1 CORINTHIANS 15:10 NLT).

While you may not be an elitist, you must guard against labeling a person or group as elitists simply because they enjoy a certain advantage that you find intimidating and alienating due to your own insecurity or in an attempt to enhance your image to others. This ploy is often used during a political campaign. A candidate may accuse his opponent of elitism simply because he has access to family wealth, graduated from a prestigious university, or has a host of high-profile, influential friends. The opponent so accused attempts to counter the charge by reaching out to blue-collar workers to prove how regular or down to earth he is.

In the final analysis, it's not what you *do* but what you *believe* that determines if you have an elitist attitude. I knew a mental health professional who had little regard for the advice of lay counselors. She believed that one had to be a licensed psychologist to give legitimate input.

Maybe it's time to look within. Do you feel superior to others in any aspect of your life? Perhaps you believe that being a part of a particular religious denomination puts you in a special class. Maybe your well-toned body makes you feel superior to the overweight masses. And what if you are well known in your community? Do you feel you should always be escorted to front-row seats at public gatherings? If so, it's time to bring your attitude into subjection to the Holy Spirit.

Prayer

Father, please forgive me for my sin of elitism. I'm

sorry that I've allowed my advantaged position to cause me to lose perspective of Your purpose for entrusting such favor to me. Help me from this moment forward to use it for Your glory. In the name of Jesus, I pray. Amen.

Day 9

Choose Healthy Expectations

"Why didn't you repay your mother for the car loan?" Judge Judy, the popular judge on *The People's Court* television show, quizzed the young defendant.

"Because I received a grant and she didn't have to pay my tuition as planned, so I shouldn't have to pay her the money for the car. After all, she was going to be out the money anyway if she had paid my tuition."

As viewers expected, Judge Judy gave the young lady a well-deserved tongue lashing for her entitlement attitude. Such a mindset is rampant not only among the younger generation but it is pervasive in every institution of society: corporations, government, churches, schools, families, and friendships.

Some of my close acquaintances feel entitled to my time and are annoyed when I have to schedule or put time constraints on our social gatherings. Relatives feel entitled to a personal loan or gifts from me because they assume I have the money. When I managed a staff at a large corporation, they felt entitled to Christmas gifts from me simply because I was the boss and had started the practice my first year on the job. Crown Financial Ministries calls this the U-Owe-Me versus the IOU mindset.

The common attitude today is "somebody owes me something." Many Americans think that a lifetime job with good pay and a guaranteed retirement plan at 65 come with just being born, promotion is a matter of time, 40 hours a week is the maximum endurance for any worker, the last hour of each day is there to make the transition to home easier, a 10-minute coffee break should take at least half an hour, a half-hour lunch should take at least an hour and a half, and an equal share of company profits belong to the workers.[3]

Before passing judgment on those who think this way, I took an inventory of my own entitlement attitude. Here are just a few of my entitlement rights that came to mind:

- I feel entitled to a prompt response from any of my six brothers to any reasonable request I make of them because I am always there for them no matter what. Plus, I'm their only sister.

- I feel entitled to a card, phone call, or some form of acknowledgement from my closest friends and family members on my birthday because I acknowledge theirs.

- I feel entitled to flowers from my church if I am hospitalized because of the sacrificial giving and service I have rendered (and yes, I understand that I gave to God and not to man).

I confess that in the past I have been disappointed, frustrated, or angered in all of the instances above. As I thought about each one, I realized I had elevated each *expectation* to the status of a *right*. But what gives me—or you—such a sense of entitlement? The source of the attitude is found right in the middle of the word *entitlement* itself: "title." We think that people owe us because of the *title* we hold in their lives: mother, daughter, brother, wife, friend, donor, pastor, employee, boss. We treat that title as if it were a title deed that gives us the right to whatever benefit we expect.

Some attitudes of entitlement stem not just from personal relationship titles but also from a person's status in the culture (for example, a woman feeling that a man *owes* her his seat on a crowed train) or from past inequities ("I deserve to be taken care of by the government because of past discrimination."). When people think they have a right to such benefits, they often are ungrateful to their benefactors even when they accommodate those expectations. Have you ever extended a courtesy only to have the recipient act as if you should have done so?

I'm pleased each time I read the parable of the prodigal son and how he did not exhibit an attitude of entitlement. He left home and spent his entire inheritance—which he had insisted his father give him—on partying and fast living. An economic downturn and the resulting famine forced him to face reality; "no one gave him anything" (Luke 15:16). He returned home and said to his father, "I am no longer worthy to be called your son. Make me like one of your hired servants" (Luke 15:19). He felt no entitlement to resume the good life simply because he had the title of "son." His father owed him nothing.

If you have an attitude of entitlement, here are some strategies to help you overcome this relationship-destroying mindset:

- Put each of your expectations in perspective. Ask yourself, "Is what I expect simply a *desire* or a covenantal, contractual, or constitutional *right*? Yes, I expect fidelity from my husband as part of our marriage covenant. While I also expect him to pick up heavy objects for me, I'm very clear that this is a demonstration of his love and not a covenantal right.

- Resist the role that selfishness plays in this attitude by being willing to meet the reasonable expectations of those on whom you place expectations. Remember that meeting expectations should be a two-way street.

- Don't manipulate others into meeting your expectations by making extreme sacrifices for them and then expecting them to jump at your beck and call because of it.

- Do not assume that a person's past kindness or benevolence to you sets a pattern or entitles you to ongoing benefits. Understand that he has the freedom to eliminate or delay such a practice at his discretion.

- Make it a habit to express appreciation for every act of kindness that anyone extends to you. This will serve to remind you that nobody owes you anything!

Prayer

Father, deliver me from ingratitude and self-centeredness. Help me to have healthy expectations and to abandon my sense of entitlement when it is not a contractual, covenantal, or constitutional right. In the name of Jesus, I pray. Amen.

Day 10

Choose to Believe God Is in Control

"Well, there's no sense in undergoing all those special treatments. If I'm going to die from this disease, I'm going to die. Que sera, sera; whatever will be, will be."

Perhaps you have heard someone express this attitude when faced with a difficult life decision. The belief that the events of our lives are predetermined, set in stone, and beyond our control is called fatalism—and it is not biblical although certain Scriptures seem to imply support for this concept. For example, Psalm 139:16 (NLT) declares,

> You saw me before I was born.
> > Every day of my life was recorded in your book.
> Every moment was laid out
> > before a single day had passed.

Do you think this is a license to live your life with no personal responsibility for how it turns out? Absolutely not! God has made us stewards not only over our money but over every aspect of our lives. Do you really believe that since God has determined the number of days that you will live you have no obligation to ensure the *quality* of those days by taking care of your body or maintaining healthy relationships with others?

A fatalistic attitude can lead to a sense of resignation about life and rob you of godly ambition and enthusiasm about the future. "If I can't change destiny, then why bother trying?" While God in his foreknowledge knows every decision we will make from cradle to grave, He has not predetermined them. He has given every person a free will. Even where we will spend eternity will be based upon the choices we make. These choices include not only making Jesus Lord over our lives but also a decision to embrace the Word of God as the foundation and reference point for every aspect of our existence.

In describing the great white throne judgment we all will face, John reported, "And I saw the dead, small and great, standing before God, and books were opened. And another book was opened, which is the Book of Life. And the dead were judged *according to their works*, by the things which were written in the books" (Revelation 20:12, emphasis added).

Yes, God is sovereign and rules in the affairs of men. I believe He has designed a wonderful plan for my life and yours. If we acknowledge Him and submit to His guidance, we will fulfill our divine destiny. However, being human, we are subject to doing things according to our own understanding and veering from His ordained path.

In times like these, God, because of His love and mercy, responds in a manner similar to the global positioning system (GPS) on today's vehicles. On a recent road trip, I programmed the GPS for my destination. However, on the way there, I got a bright idea for a quick shopping detour and made an unscheduled turn. The automated GPS voice immediately said, "Recalculating..." and proceeded to tell me how to get back on the path that would get me to my original destination. No, the brakes on the car did not lock, neither did the alarm sound. I simply had to make a choice to ignore or heed the new instructions.

Is there a circumstance in your life that you have surrendered to fate? Perhaps you've said, "I'm destined to be fat; it's in my genes!" "It's not in the cards for me to have financial abundance." "I'm just shy; that's how God made me." Don't let your fatalistic attitude sentence you to a life of excuses, frustration, and mediocrity.

Yes, God has set the framework of your life, but He has given you a wide range of freedoms within that framework. Like a GPS, God knows exactly where you are in life and what you need to do to fulfill your divine destiny. Why not stop right now and acknowledge an area where your fatalism is reigning unchecked and ask God to give you a specific strategy for overcoming this mindset.

Prayer

Lord, I acknowledge You as the sovereign ruler over my life. Help me to hear Your voice. Give me the courage to obey Your instructions for conquering my fatalistic attitude. In the name of Jesus, I pray. Amen.

Day 11

Choose to Be Pleasant

Ding-dong...Ding-dong...Ding-dong.
"Who in the world could that be?" I muttered.

I glanced at the clock and saw that it was only 7 a.m. I had gone to bed after 3 a.m. and had planned to sleep at least seven hours. I peeked out the window only to see the gardener standing at the front door with a sheepish look on his face. He had forgotten his key to the backyard security gate—again. I barreled downstairs, grabbed my spare key from the windowsill, and handed it to him without a word. I'm sure he thought, *Grumpy broad!* I justified my actions by concluding that grumpiness is not my usual demeanor.

Are you generally in a good mood and make it a point to respond pleasantly to others most of the time? It is one thing to have an occasional incident like the one above that causes you to show irritation, but a pattern of being irritable, moody, or out of sorts is a sign that your life is out of balance. Further, those in your circle of interaction will find it difficult to relate to you—much like trying to hug a porcupine.

As with any negative behavior, the first step to overcoming it is to acknowledge the problem. Notice I didn't say *justify* the problem. Simply be truthful with yourself as you replay your most recent encounters with others. Do you need to take corrective action? Here are a few surefire strategies that will bring you into the land of the pleasant.

- *Pray immediately upon arising.* Don't wait until you are bombarded with the stressors of the day; get God on your side first thing. Ask Him to infuse you with His peace and joy and to empower you to respond His way throughout the day. Remember "the joy of the LORD is your strength" (Nehemiah 8:10).

- *Get adequate sleep.* In my book, *30 Days to Taming Your Stress*, I explain: "Most of us think of sleep as some passive process in which we drift off into oblivion and wake up several hours later hopefully being more rested. The truth of the matter is that sleep is a very active state. Many metabolic and other restorative processes occur during the various stages of sleep. If we do not sleep long enough for our system to be rejuvenated, we will most likely find ourselves irritated by the smallest things."[4]

- *Get a medical checkup.* You may be a "pain in

the neck" due to a literal pain in the neck or other parts of your body. My otherwise fun-loving husband was constantly grumpy when he battled with cluster headaches. With proper medication, the excruciating attacks subsided and he returned to his formerly fun self.

- *Exercise.* Even a short period of stretching, walking, or other forms of exercise can affect your mood by raising the endorphins ("feel good" hormones) in your brain. Get outside and inhale fresh air if at all possible. Try a group exercise class for even more benefits.

- *Watch your diet.* Too much caffeine, sugar, or refined foods will negatively affect your mood. If you must indulge, be sure to combine a "bad" snack choice with some healthy protein (cheese, turkey, nuts) to slow down the absorption of the sugar into your bloodstream and to prevent a spike in your insulin.

- *Say yes to requests for personal favors only when you want to.* This will prevent you from becoming overloaded and resentful regarding work dumped on you by others.

- *Plan a social activity with positive friends.* Stay away from negativity. "Do not be deceived: 'Evil company corrupts good habits'" (1 Corinthians 15:33).

- *Focus on the needs of others.* There is nothing like bringing light and hope to the less fortunate to change your grumpy attitude. When I teach self-development classes at the local homeless shelter for women, I reap huge emotional dividends. It just feels like the right thing to do.

- *Dig deeper.* If none of the above strategies help your grumpiness, look deeper into your soul and be honest about what's really irritating you. Do you need to confront an inequity? Frustrated with your lack of direction? What's really going on with you? If necessary, talk to a counselor or someone who knows you well.

Prayer

Father, I really desire to represent You by modeling Your love and warmth in the world. Deliver me from grumpiness. Reveal the root cause of it and give me the courage to take the actions necessary to keep it out of my life. In the name of Jesus, I pray. Amen.

Day 12

Choose to Think Positively of Others

When Donna entered the church sanctuary, the usher handed her a three-fold brochure that featured prayers and affirmations prepared by Pastor Joe. He was a great teacher and the information would surely prove helpful in the upcoming weeks. However, the only thing Donna could focus on was that the folded brochure opened inwardly rather than outwardly.

What incompetent did this? she thought as she was ushered to her seat. As soon as she sat down, she proceeded to fold the brochure correctly—the way brochures are "supposed" to be. Of course, her new fold threw the page sequence off. So she took out her pen and renumbered the pages. She made a mental note to call the church staff to prevent this from happening again.

The worship team had already begun singing the morning hymn. Donna immediately noticed the unflattering fit and inappropriate skirt lengths that some of the female team members wore. *They need to wear uniforms,* she mused. *Their appearance is distracting!*

After what Donna judged as several unnecessary, time-consuming announcements, Pastor Joe finally took the pulpit and began his message. Within minutes, the microphone started to screech and finally went silent. This was becoming a recurring annoyance on Sunday mornings. *Good Lord,* Donna thought, *when are they going to fix that sound system?*

The service ended and Donna left feeling the entire endeavor had been one big waste of time. Despite the life-changing principles Pastor Joe had taught, she had felt no connection to God that day. Even though she had not verbalized her observations to anyone, Donna's faultfinding had sabotaged her experience.

I can relate to Donna for I have a tendency to judge other people's poor choices, shortcomings, and inefficiencies. It just seems hard to overlook behavior that doesn't line up with what I think reflects excellence or what "should" be. I'm on a campaign to banish this attitude from my life.

A critical attitude has at least three negative consequences.

First of all, it is a sin. When Aaron and Miriam, Moses' brother and sister, criticized him for marrying an Ethiopian woman, God judged them by striking Miriam with leprosy, the dreaded disease of the day that immediately made her a social outcast. Aaron was quick to repent. "So Aaron said to Moses, 'Oh, my lord! Please do not lay this sin on us, in which we have done foolishly and in which we have sinned'" (Numbers 12:11). Moses prayed that God would heal Miriam, and God immediately answered his prayer. But she had to face the consequences discussed below.

Second, our sin of a critical attitude can isolate us from cherished relationships. "Then the LORD said to Moses, 'If her father had but spit in her face, would she not be shamed seven days? Let her be shut out of the camp seven days and afterward she may be received again'" (Numbers 12:14). The laws regarding lepers required this separation. A critical spirit is relational leprosy, and we may find people treating us accordingly.

When my 11-year-old niece sent me an email, I was delighted; however, it contained several spelling and grammatical errors. I took the liberty of correcting each one and sending her the corrections. I told her that I wanted to turn our emails into a learning experience for her. I haven't received another email from her since! I'm not naïve as to why this may be so. People embrace those who accept them "as is"; no one enjoys being under the constant eye of a critic. This doesn't mean that we never give constructive feedback. However, we need to lean more toward affirmation and encouragement and to address only matters of serious concern.

Third, a critical attitude hinders our progress and that of others in our circle of interaction. Miriam's isolation brought the entire pilgrimage to the Promised Land to a temporary halt. "So Miriam was shut out of the camp seven days, and the people did not journey till Miriam was brought in again" (Numbers 12:15).

Have you ever been a part of an organization where one faultfinding person destroyed the effectiveness or progress of the entire group? Or what about the critical parent or spouse who so destroys the confidence of a child or mate that he or she never develops the coping or survival skills to move forward in life.

If that critical person is you, let's see if we can identify the root cause of your behavior and how you can eliminate it from your life. What makes us critical? A critical spirit is learned behavior. Here are a few of the reasons why some have such a spirit:

- Many critical people were raised by parents or others who had no clue how to affirm another person—so they never saw it modeled. Some parents erroneously believe that being critical inspires a child to achieve great success.

- Sometimes, because of our unique gifting or experience, we don't stop to consider that our talents and experience are indeed unique to us—and given by the grace of God. Thus, we unwisely expect everyone else to measure up to our level.

- Pride and arrogance because of past successes can also cause us to think that we know what is best for all; down with the "idiots" who do not do things "our" way.

- Our unresolved anger and hurt over past incidents (or just plain envy) can cause us to harbor resentment toward some people and to use every opportunity to diminish their image in the eyes of others.

- Finally, a critical spirit is often an unconscious attempt to hide our own faults and shortcomings by casting a negative light on others. I challenge you to stop now and think of the person, group, or organization you are most critical of and consider whom you criticize them to. Are you trying to increase your stature in the eyes of others?

The Cure

- Know what God's Word says about a critical spirit: "Judge not, that you be not judged. For with what judgment you judge, you will be judged; and with the same measure you use, it will be measured back to you" (Matthew 7:1-2). Do you really want to reap the consequences of planting such a negative seed?

- Acknowledge and repent of the sin of judging or faultfinding. If this is a habit in your family, determine that by the power of the Holy Spirit, the trend stops with you.

- Look for admirable qualities in those you criticize, especially qualities you may not possess. I once had a client who had an incompetent employee whose performance I always found myself criticizing. When I started to look for his good qualities, I realized that he had a teachable spirit and readily admitted

his mistakes—versus my tendency to ratio-
nalize away my mistakes or to blame others.
I also pondered if I was unconsciously trying
to enhance my image as "Super Woman" in
the client's eyes.

- Commit to extending to others the grace and
  mercy God extends to you daily. "Blessed
  are the merciful, for they shall obtain mercy"
  (Matthew 5:7).

Prayer

Lord, help me to appreciate and acknowledge the
good that every person brings to the table. Let Your love
flow through me and cause me to overlook a multitude
of faults. In the name of Jesus, I pray. Amen.

Day 13

Choose to Be Patient

"So what's the bottom line?" Jill wanted to shout at the woman who was giving the support group the long version of her current dilemma. It was getting late, and five members were still waiting for their turn to share the issues they had faced during the week.

As a trained counselor, Jill knew she had to resist the urge to show her impatience. Sure she was high-strung and impatient in general, but she'd recently had an "aha" moment during a Bible study at church. She had finally gotten it: patience is a *fruit* of the Holy Spirit. It wasn't something that she could achieve through a New Year's resolution or by counting to ten; it could be *produced* in her only by the Spirit of God—with her cooperation.

Perhaps you, along with me, share Jill's challenge in this area. In my quest to understand the root cause of my tendency to become impatient with others, I reminded myself that we are all a product of a fast-paced, instant gratification society where we have become accustomed to instant communication (phone, texting, instant messaging), instant food, instant credit, instant news, high-speed Internet, and a host of other "now" conveniences that cause us to become annoyed at waiting for *anything*. Our impatience has far-reaching consequences since it affects us physically, emotionally, and relationally. We need a major shift in our expectations regarding how fast we should move or the pace at which we expect others to do so.

I've decided, for starters, to take control over the physical impact of impatience. The minute I feel the anxiety and the corresponding (very harmful) adrenaline rush, I acknowledge this insidious enemy and take full responsibility for its cause and my response.

For example, sometimes I feel impatience rear its ugly head when I'm helping my mom and her elderly friends get into my vehicle. Often my mind is focused on the rest of the day's tasks and the limited time that I have to complete them. As these women move at a snail's pace, I have learned to call upon God for His help, breathe deeply, lower my expectation, and make a mental note to prioritize the day differently next time. I also thank God that they are alive and that I have the opportunity to serve them. I also acknowledge when my poor planning and ineffective time management have played a role in organizing the day.

I try to use a similar strategy in every "waiting" situation I encounter. Why should I become perturbed with the grocery checker, the bank teller, or the slow driver because she doesn't move at warp speed? Why not prepare to wait by keeping a book or magazine (or CD in the car) handy? Further, I also believe delays are often part of divine protection. I heard stories of people who escaped the destruction of the September 11 terrorist attack on the World Trade Center simply because they were delayed for various reasons in getting to work. I'm sure most were perturbed with the delay at the time it occurred.

Impatience affects us emotionally since we feel angry and exasperated when things do not go the way we think they should. Our ability to endure delays without emotional interference will preserve our joy and keep us at peace.

Impatience hurts our relationships in that it causes us to relate to others in a nonbeneficial, noncompassionate manner. Think about how you feel when even a stranger is short-tempered with you. Depending on your spiritual maturity, you either want to retaliate or run from his presence. If this person is significant to you and you value his perception of you, his impatience can rob you of your confidence and make you feel devalued. Remember this when you are tempted to express your impatience even in the form of a deep sigh.

Once when I managed an extremely incompetent staff member in whom I had invested endless hours in training and development, I found myself sighing in his presence to express my disappointment with his performance. What I did not realize at the time was that, rather than motivating him, my response decreased his effectiveness even more. His anxiety increased causing his emotions to sabotage his ability to think clearly.

Overcoming impatience begins with an awareness of its presence, a commitment to allow the Holy Spirit to produce patience in you, and a decision to stay in the present moment rather than obsessing about what must happen next or later.

Prayer

Father, I am so grateful for the patience that You show toward me each day. I ask that You help me to extend it to others so that they will see Your love in me and glorify You. In the name of Jesus, I pray. Amen.

Day 14

Choose to Be Happy for Others' Good Fortune

Can you handle success? No, not yours; someone else's? Perhaps everyone at some time or another has observed the good fortune of a person and felt discontentment and even resentment. I know I have.

Just a few weeks ago I turned my TV to a popular daytime show and there was Ms. X spouting her financial wisdom. I had to admit that she gave sound advice, but when her name came up in our financial Bible study group that night, I found delight in saying, "I love her advice also. Too bad she's not a Christian."

Most of the people at the Bible study were aware of this and were rather apathetic about it. What bothered me later was why I had been so eager to mention this fact. Perhaps it was because one of the members was going on and on about how awesome Ms. X was and how much she admired her. Yes, I did indeed admire her; however, what I thought was, *It isn't fair that she has reached such fame and fortune. I deserve that. I'm a Spirit-filled committed*

Christian, a submitted wife, and a faithful tither. Yes, I've achieved some level of success, but nothing compared to Ms. X. She's a media darling! I was ashamed at the carnality of my thinking as I reflected on it later.

When you practice being honest with yourself, the best place to run is to the Scriptures for more revelation and cleansing. That's exactly what I did. The light of God's Word exposed an area that most of us are loath to admit. Envy had reared its head. I thought I had completely slain it eons ago.

What causes an envious attitude? Why do we often criticize someone who has what we desire? And why do we try to tie God's hands from blessing those we feel do not deserve it? What does the Bible say about envy anyway? Is it really a sin or just an unproductive character trait?

Lucifer, whom God had appointed to lead the heavenly host of angels, became envious of God and wanted the worship and adoration God received.

> *"How you are fallen from heaven,*
> *O Lucifer, son of the morning!...*
> *For you have said in your heart:*
> *'I will ascend into heaven,*
> *I will exalt my throne above the stars of God...*
> *I will ascend above the heights of the clouds,*
> *I will be like the Most High.'"*
> (ISAIAH 14:12-14)

This is our attitude when we envy others. We want the admiration and worship they receive because of the thing they possess. We believe we can be esteemed only if we have what they have.

The last of the Ten Commandments, "You shall not covet…" (Exodus 20:17), warns us not to desire anything that someone else possesses. Such an attitude in essence accuses God of being unfair, a respecter of persons, and unaware of what is best for our lives. Therefore, we would be wise to wage an all-out campaign against envy when it shows up in our life. Here's how:

- Confess and repent of your impure motives for desiring something other than for the glory of God. "But if you harbor bitter envy and selfish ambition in your hearts, do not boast about it or deny the truth" (James 3:14 NIV).

- Count your blessings. Envy is rooted in discontentment, and often we are so pained at the good fortune of others that we are blinded to our own advantages. Someone once said, "Envy is the habit of counting someone else's blessings instead of your own."

- Understand what your envy is telling you about the decisions, training, and other actions you need to take to fulfill your destiny. Accept that looks or family heritage are beyond your control. Ask God for clarity of His will for you.

- Spend time, if possible, with the person you envy to find out more about her and her secrets to success. You may find that she has a host of problems that will curb your envy. A colleague I envied many years ago for her extraordinary beauty told me of her painful childhood abandonment and her battle with insecurity. She confessed that she envied me for my courage to confront thorny issues with intimidating folks. I was shocked.

- Rather than making negative comments, speak words of admiration when someone praises someone you are tempted to envy.

- Refuse to view another person's success as your failure.

Prayer

Lord, please help me to trust You enough to believe that You give me what I need for every season of my life and that my destiny is in Your hands. Help me to put away vain ambitions and to be genuinely happy for the good fortune of another, for You are no respecter of persons. In the name of Jesus, I pray. Amen.

Day 15

Choose to Walk in Humility

As I headed to the parking lot, I mused, "Today I'll finally get my opportunity to shine." After years of doing the detailed analyses, what-if scenarios, and other grunt work with little or no recognition, I was finally invited by senior management to the venture capital financing meeting with our coinvestors. The deal was complicated, and I knew that I understood it better than my male associates, which I was certain was the reason I was invited.

I personally made copies of the presentation to guard against any potential collating glitches by my assistant and carefully placed them in my computer bag. I checked my appearance in the office mirror. I wore a professional, cream-colored silk suit I was able to button with ease and great pride since I'd just come off my latest crash diet—down 15 pounds!

Now our investment partners will see who the real brain

is behind these deals, I thought. I was overwhelmed with excitement—and pride.

As I backed out of the parking stall, I felt my tires roll over something. When I stopped to check what had happened, to my dismay I discovered that I had left my computer bag behind the car and had backed over it! The bag was crushed almost completely flat. While the computer miraculously remained intact, the crumpled papers now resembled tostada bowls. In my effort to collect the contents of the bag, I got tire grime all over my suit. There was no time left to do anything except get to the meeting. By the time I arrived, I was so humiliated I selected a chair in a remote corner of the room and hardly said anything the entire meeting. I had gone from haughtiness to humility in three minutes.

This incident happened over 20 years ago, and I'll never forget the lesson I learned:

> *Pride goes before destruction*
> *And a haughty spirit before a fall.*
> (PROVERBS 16:18)

Since then, I have seared John 15:5 into my mind and spirit: "I am the vine, you are the branches. He who abides in Me, and I in him, bears much fruit; *for without Me you can do nothing*" (emphasis added). I remind myself of this every time I undertake any endeavor. I believe it with all my heart. It keeps me emotionally grounded and spiritually balanced. I have no reason to feel inadequate, nor am I tempted to become cocky with self-confidence.

Of all the destructive attitudes discussed in this book, haughtiness is among the worst. Why? Because God hates it (Proverbs 6:16-17). It robs Him of His glory when we attempt to take credit for what we could not have done without Him—which is everything.

What is the object of your pride? Is it your possessions? Your place in society? Your position on your job? Your profits from your profession? Do you really believe you got these things on your own? "For who makes you differ from another? And what do you have that you did not receive? Now if you did indeed receive it, why do you boast as if you had not received it?" (1 Corinthians 4:7).

Once you commit to ridding haughtiness from your life, use the strategies below to jumpstart your efforts:

- Ask the Holy Spirit to change your fundamental beliefs about who you are and what you can do. Meditate on the aforementioned Scriptures and allow them to become part of your spiritual fiber.

- In conversation, focus your attention on the interest of others and speak less of yourself.

- Respect the inherent value of every human being without regard to his social status, race, gender, or other distinguishing factors. When I met Pastor Rick Warren (author of *The Purpose Driven Life*) several years ago, I was immediately impressed with his humility. Despite the line of people waiting to talk to him, he gave me a big hug, willingly took a picture with me, and at my request, prayed a quick blessing over my book, *30 Days to Taming Your Tongue.*

And what, you may ask, is it going to buy you once you start to walk in humility?

- *Love and admiration.* Haughtiness and pride repel, but people love and admire those who demonstrate humility. It is the topmost admired character trait in the world.

- *Personal peace.* Those who have humbled themselves and submitted to their God-ordained destiny have nothing to prove—no anxiety surrounds the protection of their ego or image.

- *Trust and respect.* Because humble people look out for the good of others, people respect their input and decisions and do not suspect them of selfish motives.

Prayer

Father, I'm sorry for trying to steal Your glory. Teach me how to walk in humility that I may inspire others to follow my example. In the name of Jesus, I pray. Amen.

Day 16

Choose Tolerance

We all have a thing or two we can't tolerate. I can't stand for people to chew loudly. I tend to avoid poor communicators who get upset or emotional when somebody does not share their opinion. It irks me when women dress inappropriately for church. It annoys me when preachers and public speakers consistently mispronounce words or use incorrect grammar.

Yes, I admit that I have a pretty extensive list. These kinds of intolerances are fairly common and mostly harmless to others. In my case, they are a reflection of my unwillingness to extend to others the grace that God extends to me. I've made tremendous progress, but this is an area I consistently target in prayer.

The intolerance that we'll discuss in this chapter is more troublesome to society and to our souls. It is that mean-spirited, hate-filled rejection of people created in God's image simply because they have chosen a certain lifestyle, a particular political affiliation, a religious belief, or other views that we strongly oppose. And yes, racism is also a form of intolerance. Because of the significant impact it has had on American society, I will deal with it separately in the next chapter.

At the outset, let's clarify what tolerance is and what it is not. Tolerance is not about *agreeing to embrace* differences. It is *accepting* every person's God-given *right*, as free moral agents, to believe as he wishes and to behave according to those beliefs so long as his actions do not infringe upon the rights of others or violate established laws.

Whether we choose to love and pray for those whose beliefs and behavior we deem intolerable is a sure test of our emotional and spiritual maturity. When such beliefs violate biblical commands or principles, our response as children of God should be the same as it would be if we were to see a blind man heading for a cliff. Unfortunately today, the typical reaction is to condemn him for going in that direction rather than having compassion and showing him a safer route.

By no means should we view compassion as compromise, any more than we could accuse God, who loves sinners and hates sin, of compromise. Why don't we just emulate our heavenly Father? This does not preclude us from protesting efforts to legalize beliefs and lifestyles that violate Scripture or that we know would be detrimental to society. However, we must be careful not to address these issues with an intolerant attitude.

Let me be more specific. You can be tolerant of the homosexual hairstylist at your salon without compromising your belief that the Bible says homosexual acts are sinful. You can cooperate with your prochoice coworkers on company projects while being adamantly opposed to abortions. You can respect that your neighbor is a Democrat without ostracizing him as a "bleeding heart liberal" because you are a conservative Republican. You can honor the emotional display during the worship services of certain charismatic churches without judging them to be without substance—merely because you prefer worship services that are more subdued.

Intolerance is not good for society, as evidenced by the resulting crimes, riots, wars, and acts of terrorism, and it's not good for us as individuals. A certain level of agitation and nitpicking accompanies an intolerant attitude. They rob us of our joy and snuff out our light to the world. We would all be wise to heed the words of the late Dr. Edwin Cole who said, "In matters of taste, bend with the wind. In matters of principle, be as firm as a rock."

You can choose to address your intolerant attitude this very moment. Understand that seemingly harmless intolerances, such as the ones I listed at the beginning of this chapter, can create a barrier between you and those God may desire to reach. Ask God to show you when you are attempting to force people to think, act, or believe the way you do. Consider that your own thinking may be flawed in some instances.

Further, when you encounter one of your intolerable targets, be conscious of your negative feelings and consciously resist them. Ask God to replace them with care and concern. In some matters of preference (versus moral standards), you may need to change your beliefs.

Such was the case with Peter. When Cornelius the Gentile summoned him to his home, Peter was extremely reluctant to go. He explained, "You know how unlawful it is for a Jewish man to keep company with or go to one of another nation. But God has shown me that I should not call any man common or unclean" (Acts 10:28). God was uprooting embedded traditions and opening up new opportunities for the gospel. Peter continued, "In truth I perceive that God shows no partiality. But in every nation whoever fears Him and works righteousness is accepted by Him" (Acts 10:34-35). Could it be that God wants to expand the borders of your mind for His glory?

Prayer

Father, I repent of every type of intolerance that I have engaged in. Please keep me mindful that You have given every human being the right to choose his beliefs and lifestyle. I ask for an abundance of Your love and grace so that I may extend them to those who need it most. In the name of Jesus, I pray. Amen.

Day 17

Choose to Embrace
Racial Equality

Racism remains a sensitive subject. It is the proverbial elephant in the room that most would prefer not to discuss. Unfortunately, the "room" is society in general. And though great strides have been made over the past decades, the elephant didn't leave the room when the United States inaugurated its first African-American president in January 2009.

Whether it was Miriam and Aaron's criticism of Moses for marrying an Ethiopian (Numbers 12:1) or the bitter relationship between the Jews and the Samaritans (John 4:9), racism has been the scourge of mankind almost since the beginning. It seems odd that this is the case—especially among Christians—since the Bible clearly states that God made the entire human race in His own image and likeness (Genesis 1:26).

There really is only one race—the human race. Now if God in His infinite wisdom decided that each ethnicity within the human race should have its own distinguishing features, such as skin color, hair texture, and so forth, who are we to decide that those features make one race superior or inferior to another? Anyone who has a beef with such things really has a beef with God the creator and is guilty of rejecting His handiwork.

Perhaps you have a racist attitude because you had a negative experience with a person of another ethnicity. Are you really going to color an entire race with the actions of one ungodly person or a small group?

Many years ago my husband ordered a slice of his favorite cake at a restaurant. When he attempted to eat it with the same fork he had used to eat his fish entrée, he became nauseated. It was such a negative experience for him, he refused to eat fish for over 15 years. He hated it because he always associated it with nausea. I would often joke with him that I found it odd that he did not stop having dessert nor did he stop using forks! As he became more health conscious, he realized the benefits of eating fish, so he decided to give fish another chance. At first, he could stand to eat only fried fish or a specific type of fish. Later, he went beyond his comfort zone and experimented with a variety of fish entrées until he was finally able to enjoy the taste and benefits of fish prepared in different ways.

You may have to take this same approach if you are plagued with a racist attitude and desire to overcome it. Yes, a negative experience may have left a bad taste in your mouth. However, you're going to have to be proactive and to understand the spiritual and emotional freedom of having the right attitude toward all of God's creation.

Emotions follow behavior. If you start behaving differently toward people that you historically despised, your feelings are sure to change. Try these strategies and you may find your disdain for a particular ethnic group turning into acceptance:

- Memorize Galatians 3:28: "There is neither Jew nor Greek, there is neither slave nor free, there is neither male nor female; for you are *all* one in Christ Jesus" (emphasis added).

- Smile genuinely and ask God to flow His love through you.

- Be the first to say hello.

- Engage in a conversation; remember that you really do share the same concerns, such as finances, family, and health.

- Invite someone to join you in a social activity or Bible study.

  A young black couple shared with me recently that they feel isolated in their white church because those around them do not reach out to them. I challenged them to take the initiative and reach out first—and if that didn't yield the desired response, to move on to another target. Many whites are often afraid their well-meaning efforts will be rejected or misunderstood. Some simply do not know how to relate to blacks or other minorities because they have been programmed since childhood to hold certain beliefs. So they remain in their shell.

The understanding and the tearing down of the walls of racism must begin with spiritually mature and courageous people—those who are filled with and controlled by the Holy Spirit.

- Research the biographies of people of the disdained race who have made great contributions to society or have sacrificed for great causes—and do not conclude they were merely an exception to your biased thinking.

- If you are a black person who resents white people and refuses to forgive the racial atrocities and inequities of the past, consider the many whites who marched alongside Dr. Martin Luther King Jr. in the struggle for equality for blacks. They risked their lives, were incarcerated, rejected by many fellow whites, and endured much suffering. Yet they marched. In his famous "I Have a Dream" speech, Dr. King paid tribute to them. "The marvelous new militancy which has engulfed the Negro community must not lead us to a distrust of all white people, for many of our white brothers, as evidenced by their presence here today, have come to realize that their destiny is tied up with our destiny. And they have come to realize that their freedom is inextricably bound to our freedom. We cannot walk alone."

• Repent and ask God to forgive you and to rid you of the insidious attitude of racism. Constantly rehearsing the ills and inequities you may have suffered at the hands of a person of another race will only reinforce your negativity and hinder you from reaching your destiny.

Prayer

Father, forgive me for the sin of racism. Cleanse me of this evil attitude and work in me to will and to do what pleases You as I embrace and accept all ethnic groups as Your wonderful creation. In the name of Jesus, I pray. Amen.

Day 18

Choose Flexibility

"A flexible person is a happy person," my husband said, mimicking the expression I always use to adjust my attitude when my precious plans go awry. This was his way of letting me know that something had just gone wrong, but that he was putting forth an effort to "go with the flow."

While I haven't "arrived," I have made great strides in overcoming my rigid attitude. I used to put my plans in cement, and woe unto anybody who changed them. I would most likely strike their names off my list for any future interaction. Thank God for deliverance.

Over 20 years ago, the wife of a long-time friend of mine joined him on one of his revival trips to Los Angeles. When her flight arrived, she learned that her luggage had been lost. The revival service would start shortly. I'm sure she had planned to wear a special outfit, but she showed no frustration or disappointment. Her flexibility and peacefulness affected me in a profound way. I decided then that I would make every effort to become a flexible person. In fact, I renew my commitment each time I observe someone at the height of frustration simply because he refuses to be flexible.

Ray is a typical example. His job as a city maintenance worker requires him to share a truck with another man I'll call Jack. Jack tends to get extremely hot and requires the windows in the vehicle to remain down, even when it's chilly outside. Ray often finds the discomfort unbearable and infuriating. He has confronted Jack several times; company management refuses to get involved. When I counseled him recently, I asked, "Why don't you just take a heavier jacket to work? Jack obviously has a medical condition that causes his problem, and there's a limit to the level of clothing he can peel off." At first, Ray was stuck on the fact that it just "should not be so." When I pointed out that he was experiencing the most emotional turmoil—typical of inflexible people—he realized that he could continue to live in "Shouldville" or he could simply make the necessary changes.

Someone once said, "Blessed are the flexible, for they shall not be bent out of shape." Such was the case with Naaman, the commander of the Syrian army, who was afflicted with leprosy. His wife's maid, a Jewish captive, suggested that he visit the prophet Elisha to seek healing. He had envisioned the healing scenario before he left home. However, when he arrived, Elisha didn't even bother to come out and greet him.

> But Elisha sent a messenger out to him with this message: "Go and wash yourself seven times in the Jordan

*River. Then your skin will be restored, and you will be
healed of your leprosy."*

*But Naaman became angry and stalked away. "I
thought he would certainly come out to meet me!" he
said. "I expected him to wave his hand over the leprosy
and call on the name of the LORD his God and heal me!
Aren't the rivers of Damascus, the Abana and the Pharpar,
better than any of the rivers of Israel? Why shouldn't I
wash in them and be healed?" So Naaman turned and
went away in a rage* (2 KINGS 5:10-12 NLT).

Even in his needy condition, Naaman clung to his
rigid attitude. Had it not been for the wise intervention of his servants, who encouraged him to at least try
what the prophet had said, he would not have received
his healing. Fortunately, he adjusted his attitude, and
after his seventh dip in the dirty Jordan River, his leprosy disappeared.

Do you resist change and insist on your expectations? If so, find a quiet place and reflect on the following questions:

- What are the unknowns that I fear about this
  change or deviation in plans?

- If none of the things I fear could happen,
  how could this change improve the quality
  of my life spiritually, relationally, emotionally,
  financially, or physically?

- Am I willing to risk God's perfect will by

resisting a change He is orchestrating? Your inflexibility is an attempt to control an outcome. Many miss God's best because, like Naaman, they have put Him in a box and are looking only inside the box for their answer. Force yourself to look outside the box by being flexible.

- Am I being lazy or complacent and not wanting to invest the necessary time and effort into the change?

Start to embrace a different way of doing something, even simple things, each day (e.g., go a different way to work, sit in a different section at church, interact with a person you don't know). Also, try meditating on these quotes from great men regarding change:[5]

- "Every human has four endowments: self-awareness, conscience, independent will and creative imagination. These give us the ultimate human freedom—the power to choose, to respond, to change" (Steven Covey).

- "Change is the law of life. And those who look only to the past or present are certain to miss the future" (John Fitzgerald Kennedy).

- "The world hates change yet it is the only thing that has brought progress" (Charles Franklin Kettering).

- "One cannot manage change. One can only be ahead of it" (Peter F. Drucker).

Prayer

Lord, help me to acknowledge You in all my ways so You can direct my path. Give me the emotional and spiritual strength to embrace every change that You have destined for me to achieve Your purpose. In the name of Jesus, I pray. Amen.

Day 19

Choose to Serve with Gladness

She carries the weight of the world on her shoulders—and she makes sure everyone knows she does.

"I left work early today because I had to take my elderly neighbor to the doctor. He has no relatives in town."

"I'm so exhausted. I worked 16 hours on that proposal while the rest of the executives sauntered off to happy hour."

"I had to clean the entire house by myself in preparation for our holiday guests. My husband and kids didn't lift a finger to help me."

Sound familiar? Meet the *false* martyr. She sacrifices out of a false sense of obligation and derives satisfaction and self-esteem from the sympathy and attention it brings her from others. She can be found in every segment of human relationships: marriages, companies, churches, schools, social organizations, you name it.

"But," you may ask, "isn't martyrdom a noble act? What does a *true* martyr look like anyway?"

A true martyr sacrifices his life or personal freedom in order to further a cause or belief for the benefit of many. Famous martyrs include Dr. Martin Luther King Jr., who fought for equal civil rights for the black community, and Dietrich Bonhoeffer, a Lutheran pastor and theologian, killed by the Nazis for his role in openly resisting Adolf Hitler's policies toward the Jews. Unlike the false martyr, these men gave their lives out of a pure passion for a cause. During their lifetime, they did not exalt their personal sacrifice nor wear it as a badge of honor.

A martyr attitude can have a profoundly negative effect on relationships. Others usually find the false martyr exhausting and unpleasant to be around, primarily because false martyrs complain about their service. Further, some martyrs attempt to place a guilt trip on people who do not emulate or appreciate their sacrifices. Most people will resent being manipulated in this manner.

I have had numerous discussions with a false martyr who often accuses me and my husband of being insensitive to the needy simply because we do not broadcast or whine about our benevolence to others as he does. Further, unlike him, we are strongly opposed to enabling irresponsible financial behavior. We refuse to hand out money to people just because they ask for it. He finds every reason to justify his martyr attitude.

What about you? Do you sacrifice for others hoping to gain their favor, love, or loyalty? Do you berate yourself for always putting your needs last? Do you resent certain people for taking you for granted or violating your (usually unspoken) boundaries? Do you feel deep down inside that you do not deserve the benevolence or sacrifices of others? Do you find it difficult to ask for help for fear that you will become obligated to someone? If you are ready to free yourself from this mindset, try these strategies for the next 30 days:

Serve sincerely. "Don't just pretend to love others. Really love them" (Romans 12:9 NLT). Be honest about your real objective for sacrificing for others. Only God knows your true motive, and He has given you the Bible to help you to discern it. "For the word of God is living and powerful, and sharper than any two-edged sword... and is a discerner of the thoughts and intents of the heart" (Hebrews 4:12). I suggest reading a chapter from Proverbs each morning for wisdom, guidance, and purification of your motives.

Serve silently. Stop mentioning or complaining about the sacrifices you're making. This habit may be entrenched, so you'll have to catch yourself before you indulge. This is an easy attitude to fall into if you tend to be the go-to person in most of your circles of interaction. Just today, I caught myself complaining about three different sacrifices that I had decided to make in the midst of my tight writing schedule. I stopped and reminded myself that God gives us aptitudes, skills, and resources to be used for His glory. "For everyone to whom much is given, from him much will be required; and to whom much has been committed, of him they will ask the more" (Luke 12:48). Refuse to complain about what God asks you to do—when you know for sure He is asking.

Serve selectively. Pray before you make a personal sacrifice. Be sure that it is a "God idea" and not just a "good idea" borne out of your need to be needed. By the way, I also revisited the three sacrifices mentioned above and deleted one from the list after I realized my guilt was self-imposed and not a Holy Spirit conviction. If you think you cannot make the sacrifice out of a sincere and obedient heart, or you do not feel the peace of God to proceed, pray for the courage to say no.

Prayer

Father, forgive me for not serving others out of a pure heart. Heal me of my insecurities and impure motives and help me to serve with gladness. In the name of Jesus, I pray. Amen.

Day 20

Choose to Avoid Sarcasm

Shortly before his execution by firing squad, the murderer James Rodgers was asked whether he had any final requests. "Why yes," he replied. "I'd like a bulletproof vest."[6] Even at the point of death, he could not resist sarcasm.

Do you regularly respond to others in a way that is opposite of what you really feel—as evidenced by your tone or body language (smirking, raising eyebrows, cocking your head to the side, sighing)? Sarcasm can ruin your relationships since its goal is usually to scorn, belittle, insult, or express irritation or disapproval. You can find it in all social interactions. Here are a few examples:

At home: Junior brings in his report card, which reflects low grades in all subjects. Dad says, "Way to go, Einstein!" Dad is expressing his frustration by saying the opposite of what he's really feeling.

In sports: The rookie baseball player strikes out—for the third time. The coach yells, "Nice going, Jack!"

Romantic relationship: John buys his wife, Sue, a pair of small diamond earrings. Sue, who had hoped for larger gems, says, "Boy, these are really going to blind people!"

As a word of caution, sarcasm is not always wrong, and there are instances of its use even in the Bible. One of the most notable incidents occurred when Elijah challenged the false prophets of Baal to call down fire to prove who the real God was. He let them go first in putting a sacrifice on an altar and calling on their god to send down fire to consume it. After several hours of watching them call upon Baal with no results, Elijah became sarcastic. "And so it was, at noon, that Elijah mocked them and said, 'Cry aloud, for he is a god; either he is meditating, or he is busy, or he is on a journey, or perhaps he is sleeping and must be awakened'" (1 Kings 18:27). In this instance, Elijah justifiably used sarcasm to show the prophets of Baal the folly of worshipping a false god. God Himself used sarcasm when he ridiculed those who took a block of wood and used half of it for fuel and the other half to make a "god" (Isaiah 44:13-20).

How has your sarcastic attitude affected your life? How do you typically respond to your recurring frustrations or irritations with others? Perhaps you have convinced yourself that you are not sarcastic at all, just witty or clever. Sarcasm is no joke despite your best attempt to disguise it with a laugh. Perhaps you are not aware that your sarcasm most likely leaves the hearer feeling diminished or devalued. This is no way to win friends or influence people. If you want to begin to address this poor communication style, the strategies below should help.

Admit your motive for being sarcastic. You may be attempting to control other people or to shame them out of behavior that you disapprove. Face it, the only person you can control is yourself. Or maybe you are trying to display your great intellect by calling attention to the deficiency of another.

Practice a more direct approach to expressing your displeasure. Posing a simple question designed to gain a better understanding will go a long way. For example, rather than asking "What in the world were you thinking?" try, "What strategy or goal did you have in mind when you made that move?" This latter statement expresses confidence that surely some forethought was applied. God will give you the right words to say if you ask Him to. "Those who are wise will find a time and a way to do what is right, for there is a time and a way for everything" (Ecclesiastes 8:5-6 NLT).

Consider the implications and consequences of what you are about to say before you say it. Ask yourself, "Will my words imply that the hearer is stupid or has poor judgment? Do they tear down or do they build?" "Do not let any unwholesome talk come out of your mouths, but only what is helpful for building others up according to their needs, that it may benefit those who listen" (Ephesians 4:29 NIV). Make sure every word passes the "benefit" test.

Consider how you would feel if someone were to say to

you what you are about to say to another. Let the Golden Rule be your guide.

Prayer

Father, I need wisdom in becoming more sensitive to what I say to others. Teach me how to be more accepting of other people's shortcomings just as You are accepting of mine. In the name of Jesus, I pray. Amen.

Day 21

Choose to Leave
Revenge to God

A popular phrase says, "Don't get mad, get even!"
I'm certain most of us will admit to at least having had
a *desire* to avenge a wrong perpetrated against us. Even
if we would never do so, we may relish the idea of somebody giving our perpetrator his just dues. I used to hate
the very thought that somebody had attempted to hurt
or disadvantage me and got away with it with no appar-
ent consequences.

The Bible is replete with vindictive characters. As I've
studied them, I realize none of their lives had a positive
ending. Consider Haman, the high-ranking Persian official who sought to exterminate the entire Jewish population because Mordecai the Jew refused to bow to him.
His carefully designed plot backfired and resulted in his
own death—and that of his ten sons—as well as the
granting of his entire estate to Mordecai (Esther 3–9).

And what about the revenge that Absalom, son of
King David, took against his half brother Amnon for

raping his beloved sister Tamar. Absalom stewed in anger for two years and finally had Amnon murdered at a sheep-shearing party that he hosted for that very purpose. In relating the horrifying event, the king's nephew explained, "Absalom has been plotting this ever since Amnon raped his sister Tamar" (2 Samuel 13:32 NLT). Absalom fled the country. Even though his father permitted him to return after several years, their relationship was never the same. Absalom later attempted to take over the throne and was killed in the long-drawn-out rebellion.

How can you guard against developing a vindictive spirit? Here are some strategies that are sure to quell your temptation to get even.

Stop vocalizing your desire for revenge.

> *Do not say, "I will do to him just as he has done*
> *to me;*
> *I will render to the man according to his work."*
> (PROVERBS 24:29)

Talking about the offense and the offender keeps the emotional wound fresh and the anger brewing. Also, continually discussing the villain is a form of retaliation as you get the satisfaction of tarnishing his image.

Put your faith in divine justice. Often a person seeks revenge because he does not believe the justice system or those in authority will adequately address the wrong. Therefore, he takes matters into his own hands. In the story of Absalom's murder of Amnon, King David became angry with Amnon at the time of the rape, but he did nothing to punish him for it. Consequently,

Absalom made a decision to redress the wrong himself. This was the beginning of his end.

Refuse to engage in any form of retaliation. Some acts of revenge may not be as severe or significant as these; however, any attempt to avenge a wrong is a violation of God's Word.

Consider what forms of retaliation you've taken to avenge a wrong. Badmouthing the perpetrator? Giving the silent treatment? Making sarcastic remarks? Pretending ignorance to avoid giving assistance on the job? Not showing up? Destroying personal property? Resorting to physical violence or verbal attacks? Taking company resources without authorization? Applying workplace rules more stringently to the offending employee than to others? Deliberately slowing your pace to frustrate the offender? Withholding sex from your spouse?

These are only a few of the behaviors you must resist. God is the only authorized avenger of wrongs. "Beloved, do not avenge yourselves, but rather give place to wrath; for it is written, 'Vengeance is Mine, I will repay,' says the Lord" (Romans 12:19).

What I know for sure, after struggling for many years with a vindictive attitude, is repaying evil for evil will not bring you satisfaction. Besides, have you considered that the person who hurt you may have genuinely changed by now? What if God held your transgressions against you forever? Finally, vindictiveness will destroy your peace of mind because it displeases God. Resist it today!

Prayer

Father, by the power of Your Spirit alone, I release any desire to get even with anybody for any reason. I want to walk in Your peace and to allow You to avenge all wrongs done against me. In the name of Jesus, I pray. Amen.

Day 22

Choose to Resist
Scarcity Thinking

"How could you sabotage our businesses like that? Why would you encourage the ladies to shop the Los Angeles wholesale district when we are here offering our wares?"

This angry vendor confronted me on behalf of the entire group of clothing vendors and, boy, were they upset with me!

Even though this incident happened over 25 years ago, I can remember almost every detail. I had been invited to speak at my church's annual ladies' conference on how to shop on a budget. The conference featured some of the female entrepreneurs from the congregation who sold jewelry, ladies' clothing, and other wares primarily out of their homes. Each had purchased a vendor booth for the one-day event. It didn't occur to me when I made the suggestion to shop the deeply discounted area downtown that our vendors would think their customer base consisted only of the ladies in our local congregation. According to my confronter, my recommendation was going to have a detrimental effect on their sales.

Stunned at her outburst, I remember thinking, *How shortsighted. What little faith!* (And a few other judgmental phrases.)

Several years later, Stephen Covey would write about such a mindset in his bestselling book, *The Seven Habits of Highly Effective People*. He called it a Scarcity Mentality. Covey explained, "Most people…see life as having only so much, as though there were only one pie out there. And if someone were to get a big piece of the pie, it would mean less for everybody else."[7] He contrasted this attitude with what he called an Abundance Mentality in which people believe there is plenty out there and enough to spare for everybody.

I've seen the Scarcity Mentality at work in every facet of human interaction, from the insecure woman who refused to share a simple cookie recipe made with a few store-bought ingredients to the budding motivational speaker who would not share the name of a supplier with a speakers networking and information sharing group I was hosting. Evidently, she viewed all the other attendees as competitors for a scarce supply of buyers—even though no one in the group shared her target market. (I struck her name off the list for future gatherings. I had no desire to forge a relationship with such a limited thinker.)

I've seen scarcity attitudes in families—my family. Just let me praise brother X to brother Y and Y will find some way to diminish the action of X, as if there isn't enough praise to go around.

This attitude was also evident in the early church.

Diotrephes, a church leader, would not allow the apostle John or other leaders to come and speak at his church. John explained why not. "Diotrephes, who loves to have the preeminence among them, does not receive us" (3 John 9). He feared the loss of his preeminence or popularity with the congregation. Could there really be a shortage of such intangibles as love, appreciation, or loyalty?

I have seen a scarcity attitude hold back many people's plans and creative ideas. Some would-be authors have abandoned their dream to write about a particular subject because someone else has already written about it. Even in writing this book, I had to resist defeating thoughts, such as, *Who needs another book on attitudes?* However, I remembered the words of a well-known writing coach, "Just write *your* book. There will be an audience for *your* book."

If you struggle with a scarcity attitude in your relationships, in your profession, or other key areas of involvement, stop and consider the implications of such a mindset. It is rooted in fear and shows distrust of the awesome power of God to supply all our needs according to His great resources. It is based upon the faulty assumption that if someone else has something, you can't have it because there is only one pie and every slice that someone else gets means less is available for you. This "you win, I lose" madness must stop now. It will make you a rotten team player because you will think that sharing diminishes your portion. This is no way to live the abundant life.

Start today to reprogram your thinking. Remind yourself that you are not in competition with anybody for anything in any area of your life. Cling to the words of Jesus, "I have come that they may have life, and that they may have it more abundantly" (John 10:10).

Prayer

Father, help me to cast down thoughts of scarcity. Show me how to help others achieve their goals by sharing my time, talents, treasure, and my relational ties. In the name of Jesus, I pray. Amen.

Day 23

Choose Not to Judge Others

My friend Debbie was raised in a denomination that taught its members that they were superior to other religious groups because they spoke in tongues and refrained from worldly behaviors such as wearing pants, going to the movies, wearing makeup or nail polish, playing sports (no kidding!), and anything else deemed fun. She later learned that some of the leaders who were most adamant about the congregants obeying these strict rules were guilty of adultery, greed, and a host of other sins.

After college, Debbie relocated to another part of the country and joined a church where she was exposed to pants-and-makeup-wearing leaders. It was all very confusing to her as she sat on the sidelines smugly judging them and the rest of the congregation for their worldly ways. However, she could not deny the power of God at work as they exercised the spiritual gifts of healing, prophecies, miracles, and other manifestations of the Spirit's power.

Finally, Debbie came to realize that many of the

convictions she held were a result of man-made traditions; others were issues of personal holiness that God
had called her to in order to fulfill His purpose in her
life. And yes, some of the members were indeed worldly
by any standard, but God had extended His grace to
them for reasons that she could not comprehend.

The Pharisees, that religious sect of the Jews who
insisted on strict adherence to the law, had a similar
mindset to Debbie's. Jesus was quick to denounce it.

> *Also He spoke this parable to some who trusted in
> themselves that they were righteous, and despised others:
> "Two men went up to the temple to pray, one a Pharisee
> and the other a tax collector. The Pharisee stood and
> prayed thus with himself, 'God, I thank You that I am
> not like other men—extortioners, unjust, adulterers, or
> even as this tax collector. I fast twice a week; I give tithes
> of all that I possess.' And the tax collector, standing afar
> off, would not so much as raise his eyes to heaven, but
> beat his breast, saying, 'God, be merciful to me a sin-
> ner!' I tell you, this man went down to his house justified
> rather than the other; for everyone who exalts himself
> will be humbled, and he who humbles himself will be
> exalted"* (LUKE 18:9-14).

From this parable, it is clear that God has more tolerance for an honest sinner than a self-righteous hypo-
crite. Yes, fasting and tithing were godly pursuits, but
God knew that the Pharisees were guilty of many sins,
including making a show of their righteousness. He
spent almost the entire twenty-third chapter of Matthew denouncing their behavior.

What "good" behavior has been a source of pride for you? Perhaps you are a hard worker who has gotten fair breaks all of your life and have never needed any government assistance. Do you negatively judge those who have? Have you ignored the fact that when you cheated on your income tax return, you forced the government to give you an involuntary subsidy? Or maybe you're proud that you have never been unfaithful to your spouse; you detest those who are sexually immoral. Are you in denial about the emotional affair at the office, the R-rated movies you watch, or that quick peek at a pornographic website?

My goal in confronting these issues is not to throw a wet blanket on our desire for righteousness but to remind us that we all have sinned and come short of God's requirements. Understand that when we feel good and righteous, it is because we are close to reaching a man-made standard versus achieving true intimacy with God. The closer we get to God the more the light of His Word illuminates the blemishes in our life, and the more we become aware of our need for His grace and mercy. When we admit our weaknesses and vulnerabilities, people feel a stronger connection to us and see us as more "relatable."

The very time that I feel like I'm batting a thousand in my spiritual life, an incident will occur that sends me running back to the altar begging forgiveness (usually for unwise words said in haste or a judgmental attitude).

Once when I worked as chief financial officer at a megachurch, one of the most well-dressed women in the congregation bounced a $10 check. I remember going into Pharisee mode: "Lord, I thank You that I am not like Sister Suzy. I have been a faithful tither for over 30 years, and my checks have never bounced because I pursue the right priorities with my money. Besides that I—"

The Lord stopped me mid-sentence. "Judge not, that you be not judged" (Matthew 7:1).

It is so easy to get off track. I believe what the Spirit is saying in moments like these is, "Listen, you can't live a godly life in your own strength, so don't be lifted up in pride about the sins you don't commit. 'For it is God who works in you both to will and to do for His good pleasure' (Philippians 2:13). Doing right doesn't emanate from your carnal nature. So be merciful and extend to others the grace the Lord extends to you."

So here is a challenge for us all. Let's stop trying to deceive others and ourselves into thinking that our self-righteousness is righteousness. We need to repent of this and all other sins daily. Refuse to judge others by our man-made standards. It is hard to embrace others and to be embraced by them when we are in judgment mode. Pray for those who violate the standards set forth in God's Word. When tempted to judge others, remember that no one can ever be *too bad* for God to use, but he can be *too good*.

The only righteousness we have is from God, and He gave it to us through the blood of Jesus Christ. We can't earn it with our good deeds.

Prayer

Father, please remind me that every act of unrighteousness is sin in Your sight and not to justify my actions nor to sit in judgment of other people's behavior. In the name of Jesus, I pray. Amen.

Day 24

Choose to Be Amiable

You have encountered it in the retail clerk who barely says hello at the checkout counter, the teenager who seems to hate life in general, or the sulky employee, wife, or boyfriend who has not learned to express their preferences, dislikes, or other wishes in a productive way. It's the sullen attitude. It is a poor communication strategy and a real frustration to others.

Of course, there is nothing new under the sun. Thus, we find several biblical characters who demonstrated a sullen attitude. Consider the story of King Ahab, who could not handle that a certain landowner rejected his request to buy a plot of land from him.

> *So Ahab went into his house sullen and displeased because of the word which Naboth the Jezreelite had spoken to him; for he had said, "I will not give you the inheritance of my fathers." And he lay down on his bed, and turned away his face, and would eat no food. But Jezebel his wife came to him, and said to him, "Why is your spirit so sullen that you eat no food?"* (1 KINGS 21:4-5).

Here we have the king of Israel pouting like a baby because he can't have his way. Of course, he was a wicked king and such conduct can be expected from those who have not submitted their lives to the will and purpose of God. (Don't miss the tragic end of this story in the chapter "Choose to Relinquish Control.")

And what about the attitude of the "good son" in the story of the prodigal son? The bad son wasted his entire inheritance and returned home, humble and broken. When the good son learned that his father was throwing a party in celebration of Mr. Wasteful's return, he grew sullen and refused to attend. "But he was angry and would not go in. Therefore his father came out and pleaded with him" (Luke 15:28-30). Once again we have a grown man sulking because he doesn't like what's going on and makes no attempt to understand all the ramifications. The father explained the significance of the event, but he did not cater to his son's sullen attitude by canceling the party. Good move!

If you have resorted to eye-rolling, door slamming, silent treatment, running away, or other passive-aggressive forms of communicating your displeasure, it's time to grow up. Mature people express their concerns rather than expect others to read their minds.

I'm going to cut you a little slack here because your sullen attitude may not be your fault entirely. Odds are that you learned it, which means you had a teacher... perhaps several teachers, such as weak parents, a weak spouse, a weak boss, or weak friends. I often say, we *teach* by what we *tolerate*. I have watched parents unwittingly teach their children that it was okay to exhibit a sullen attitude by tolerating it. In so doing, they created an environment of disrespect.

Call me old-fashioned, but when I was growing up, we were not allowed to be sullen. The consequences were immediate and much more severe than "go to your room!" But that was then.

Perhaps your spouse or girlfriend may have taught you that sullenness works by catering to your pouting to avoid the discomfort of your alienation. Expressing our needs, expectations, or disappointments in a respectful way has been a cardinal rule in my marriage for over 30 years. We believe it is unfair to do otherwise. Further, a sullen attitude opens the door for resentment, that relational termite that destroys the foundation of marriage and any other relationship.

So whether or not you were "taught" that a sullen attitude gets results, it is your responsibility to conquer it. Here's how:

- Evaluate the issue from a *total* perspective versus how it is affecting you only. Your expectations may be unreasonable or you may be unaware of what it costs to meet your need. Try asking, "What factors could hinder you from granting my request?" Seek to understand. Listen intently to the response and stay calm and respectful if you feel the need to rebut it.

- Abandon your inflexible attitude (see day 18,

"Choose Flexibility") and be willing to nego-
tiate an alternative solution.

- Submit all of your desires to God with a "nevertheless…not my will but Yours" mindset.
Understand that "No" is often God's way of
achieving a higher purpose in your life.

We will not always get everything we want. Working
through disappointment builds character. Know that
even God doesn't get everything He wants; He wants
everybody to be saved, but some people will choose not
to be. He accepts that. "The Lord is not slow in keeping
his promise, as some understand slowness. He is patient
with you, not wanting anyone to perish, but everyone
to come to repentance" (2 Peter 3:9 NIV).

Prayer

Father, forgive me for not discerning and accepting
Your will in the thing that I desire. Give me the wisdom
to express my needs with respect, to respond graciously
to disappointments, and to resist manipulating others
through sullenness. In the name of Jesus, I pray. Amen.

Day 25

Choose to Reject Helplessness

The afflicted man who had lain for many years at the pool called Bethesda in Jerusalem had every reason to feel hopeless. He had suffered from his condition for 38 long years. A number of disabled people would gather at this pool because on certain occasions an angel of the Lord would come down and stir the water, and the first person to enter the water after the stirring would be healed. Naturally, there was stiff competition from the many infirm people at the pool. Because of his limited mobility, this man had yet to win first place and had become a fixture by the pool. But that was about to change.

> *When Jesus saw him lying there, and knew that he already had been in that condition a long time, He said to him, "Do you want to be made well?" The sick man answered Him, "Sir, I have no man to put me into the pool when the water is stirred up; but while I am coming, another steps down before me"* (JOHN 5:6-7).

Good grief! Why didn't he just say, "Yes, I want to

be healed"? Why did he explain the woes of his past instead? He obviously held on to a ray of hope for he could have resigned all efforts and returned home. Could it be that he had begun to enjoy being the guest of honor at his own pity party? This man was a genuine victim. In addition to his paralysis, he suffered the great tragedy of not having a loyal friend or family member to assist him in his effort to be made whole. Scripture says, "A friend is always loyal, and a brother is born to help in time of need (Proverbs 17:17). Why was his support system conspicuously absent? I don't know the answers to these questions, but he serves as a great reminder that we should be careful to nurture our relationships.

Now this chapter is not directed toward victims of recent crimes or other tragic events but rather to those who may have been victimized in the past (e.g., spousal or parental abandonment, sexual or verbal abuse, discrimination) and have not been able to move forward. Their self-pity has become their ticket to getting the attention they desire. My message is clear: You always have the option of a different response.

Take Job, for instance. He was a good man, "blameless and upright, and one who feared God and shunned evil" (Job 1:1). He could have easily felt victimized by God, who allowed Satan to take away his children, his health, and his wealth in short order. Yet, "In all this, Job did not sin nor charge God with wrong" (Job 1:22). What a model!

Whether the beef is with God or a human being, the victim is stuck in an unresolved offense and refuses to let the emotional wound heal. French philosopher Voltaire cautioned, "The longer we dwell on our misfortunes, the greater is their power to harm us." A person with a victim's mindset stays on high alert for continued offenses by others to validate and reinforce her victimhood.

What about you? Do you want to be made well? If you are willing to admit to having this attitude, let's look at some ways that you can begin to overcome it.

- Get a new perspective on the hurtful offenses of the past. Since "all things work together for good to those who love God, to those who are the called according to His purpose" (Romans 8:28), ask God to show you what "good" can come out of your pain. When Ann, a black college student, faced extreme discrimination at the hands of her English professor, she decided she would hone her writing and communication skills to perfection. She later became a bestselling author. Today, she says she's grateful for the incident and how it shaped her destiny.

- Decide to forgive all the people who have victimized you. Consider that some people on your list may only be *perceived* victimizers since you have viewed everyone through your "victim's lens." For now, forget about *feeling* differently toward them. Forgiveness is a decision to release a relational debt; it is not an emotion.

- Solicit the support of others you trust. Give them permission to let you know when your victim attitude is rearing up when they observe you sabotaging a relationship because of your past.

- Stop giving substance and reinforcement to a victim mentality. Refuse to discuss slights or other perceived acts of victimization. "The boss doesn't like me." "My wife never supports my goals." "Everybody's raise is higher than mine." "Not one of my employees acknowledged my birthday."

- Cast down thoughts of defeat, rejection, and alienation. Let your smile, your generosity, and your genuine concern for others draw people to you.

- Take responsibility for the rest of your life by taking decisive action. Jesus told our friend from the pool of Bethesda, "Rise, take up your bed and walk" (John 5:8). Do something. Get started on your future. No more excuses!

Prayer

Father, thank You for delivering me from self-pity and a victim mentality. I'm now ready to share with others the love and support that You so generously extend to me. In the name of Jesus, I pray. Amen.

Day 26

Choose to Be An Optimist

"Pessimistic Official Trampled to Death by Starving Mob!"

These words could have been the media headline that captured the events of that day when four lepers reported to Jehoram, king of Israel, that they had stumbled upon an abundant supply of food in a deserted enemy camp—enough to save the entire city of Samaria from starvation.

The saga had begun when the Syrian king Ben-Hadad laid siege to the city and cut off all food supplies. The ensuing famine was severe. Inflation was rampant. In order to survive, people were forced to eat donkey heads and use dove droppings for their cooking fires. Two mothers even agreed to eat each other's baby, but Mother Y reneged on the verbal contract after they'd eaten Mother X's baby (see 2 Kings 6:24–7:20).

King Jehoram, exasperated that God would allow such a situation to exist, decided to take his frustration out on God's prophet Elisha. Therefore, he ordered an official to go to Elisha's house and execute him. He even accompanied his official on the trip. However, when they arrived, Elisha prophesied that the famine would be over within 24 hours with food in abundance and at greatly reduced prices. Such an economic turnaround under any circumstance seemed unbelievable—especially to a pessimist.

> So an officer on whose hand the king leaned answered the man of God and said, "Look, if the LORD would make windows in heaven, could this thing be?" And [Elisha] said, "In fact, you shall see it with your eyes, but you shall not eat of it" (2 KINGS 7:2).

Shortly thereafter, four starving but optimistic lepers decided to go and beg for food in the enemy camp. But God had caused the Syrians to hear the sound of three invading armies approaching. All the soldiers had fled for their lives on foot, leaving horses, food, clothes, weapons, and the entire camp intact. The lepers were overjoyed. After indulging themselves, they reported their findings to the king. Ironically, he responded with the same pessimistic attitude exhibited by his official. (Could it be that by his behavior he had influenced his official's attitude?)

> So the king arose in the night and said to his servants, "Let me now tell you what the Syrians have done to us. They know that we are hungry; therefore they have gone out of the camp to hide themselves in the field, saying, 'When they come out of the city, we shall catch them alive, and get into the city'" (2 KINGS 7:12).

The king dispatched a group to investigate, and they confirmed the lepers' story. The people were ecstatic—and hungry.

> *Now the king had appointed the officer on whose hand he leaned to have charge of the gate. But the people trampled him in the gate, and he died, just as the man of God had said, who spoke when the king came down to him* (2 KINGS 7:17).

The official's pessimism cost him his life.

What about you? Is pessimism robbing you of life's fullness? Has a prolonged negative experience or a series of setbacks and disappointments caused you to see only the downside of every situation? Perhaps you're not even aware of your tendency to express hopelessness about the future, belittle your own abilities or that of others, refuse to take a calculated risk, resist personal growth opportunities, complain about the unfairness of life, or to express powerlessness to make a difference in a particular circumstance. Do you want to conquer this attitude?

I'm reminded of the words of Dr. Paul Meier, popular Christian psychiatrist, "Attitudes are nothing more than habits of thoughts, and habits can be acquired. An action repeated becomes an attitude realized." The Word of God also provides practical advice for making a shift in your thinking. "Fix your thoughts on what is true, and honorable, and right, and pure, and lovely, and admirable. Think about things that are excellent and worthy of praise" (Philippians 4:8 NLT).

Overcoming pessimism requires more than a change

in thinking; you must change your behavior. For starters, you must limit or eliminate your exposure to other
pessimists. Begin to connect with optimistic people.
Perhaps I should say *reconnect* because there is a good
chance that many of your family members, coworkers, former friends, and others quietly distanced themselves from you as your pessimism continued to rear
its head. Being with a pessimist is like having a skunk
at your picnic.

You'll also want to try these additional strategies:

- Be candid with others about your quest to
  conquer pessimism. Give them permission to
  point out when you are being negative.

- Limit your exposure to negative input (media,
  movies, music).

- Volunteer to serve others who are less fortunate. Serving creates positive feelings and
  gives you a sense of value; it's also the right
  thing to do.

Yes, you can become an eternal optimist. Look for
the good in every situation and always express faith that
it is there! Remember the words of Harry S. Truman,
thirty-third president of the United States: "The pessimist is one who makes difficulties of his opportunities
and an optimist is one who makes opportunities of his
difficulties."

Prayer

Father, help me to remember that I can do all things through Christ who strengthens me—including turning pessimism into optimism. In the name of Jesus, I pray. Amen.

Day 27

Choose to Submit to Authority

From Adam and Eve to the insubordinate employee who defies the boss's orders, rebellion is in our nature. However, submission to authority is not optional for the child of God.

> *Everyone must submit to governing authorities. For all authority comes from God, and those in positions of authority have been placed there by God. So anyone who rebels against authority is rebelling against what God has instituted, and they will be punished* (ROMANS 13:1-2 NLT).

Since the passage above refers to "all authority," let's start with the family, particularly the husband and wife relationship. I must tread lightly here, but God's requirement is clear.

> *For wives, this means submit to your husbands as to the Lord. For a husband is the head of his wife as Christ is the head of the church. He is the Savior of his body, the church. As the church submits to Christ, so you wives should submit to your husbands in everything.*

For husbands, this means love your wives, just as Christ loved the church. He gave up his life for her to make her holy and clean, washed by the cleansing of God's word (EPHESIANS 5:22-26 NLT).

Spousal abuse is epidemic in our society, and many wives have become turned off by the concept of submission as harsh husbands, unwise or chauvinistic pastors, and certain counselors cite the Bible's charge only to the wife. This is a gross misapplication of Scripture. A careful reading shows that God's ideal is for wives to submit to their husbands and for husbands to love their wives sacrificially, as Christ loved the church. No husband could use this passage to justify abusing his wife.

If you are a rebellious wife, or wife-to-be, and find the whole notion of submission distasteful, I want to remind you of a few consequences of willful disobedience to this passage:

- A defiant wife robs her husband of his God-given leadership role and may motivate him to default on his responsibilities.

- By her actions a defiant wife can cause resentment, which may show up as coldness and lack of intimacy.

- A defiant wife is embarrassing and damaging to a man's self-esteem and may indeed provoke him to be harsh or abusive.

I am not justifying or condoning any of these

potential results. This is merely an admonition to be forewarned. I know a man who has proposed to a woman who was sexually abused by her father and now has a negative attitude toward submission, since her mother's submissiveness allowed the abuse to continue. He is having second thoughts about his proposal, and rightly so, since she rebels against the simplest request he makes—even in the presence of his friends—which he finds humiliating.

Defiance on the job can have dire consequences as well. Whether you were passed over for a promotion, assigned an incompetent boss, or feel that you have been treated unfairly, submission is still the order of the day. In many companies, insubordination is official justification for termination. Except for matters of legality or violation of your personal convictions, there is never a reason to resist your superior's request. Even when you must for legal or moral reasons, watch the tone and spirit in which you refuse to obey.

Note the sensitivity Daniel, the Jewish captive, used in response to the king's order to eat non-kosher food.

> *And the king appointed for them a daily provision of the king's delicacies and of the wine which he drank...*
>
> *But Daniel purposed in his heart that he would not defile himself with the portion of the king's delicacies, nor with the wine which he drank; therefore he requested of the chief of the eunuchs that he might not defile himself* (DANIEL 1:5,8).

What wisdom and finesse! Daniel was not defiant

even though he had already decided that under no circumstances was he going to comply with the order. His humble request for a vegetarian diet was granted, and all ended well.

An insubordinate attitude will buy you a one-way ticket to nowhere. (If you happen to manage an insubordinate subordinate, nip his disrespectful behavior in the bud. When insubordination is tolerated, the employee feels emboldened to continue it. Before you know it, you will have lost the respect of the rest of your staff and peers.)

Whether you are a defiant wife, employee, student, teenager, or other, know that God hates rebellion and sees it as sin. Scripture reminds us that "obedience is better than sacrifice, and submission is better than offering the fat of rams. Rebellion is as sinful as witchcraft, and stubbornness as bad as worshiping idols" (1 Samuel 15:22-23 NLT).

As you consider your tendency to be defiant, try to uncover and understand the root cause, which may include one of more of the following:

- painful history of suffering or being victimized

- disrespect for an incompetent superior

- pride because of your superior skills

- unfair treatment from those in authority

- ploy to test the sincerity, care, or concern of an authority figure

Commit today to ridding yourself of the evil of a defiant attitude. Stop and pray about your response when tempted to rebel.

> *Evil people are eager for rebellion,*
> *but they will be severely punished.*
> (PROVERBS 17:11 NLT)

Haven't you been "punished" long enough for your defiance (loss of a job, loss of promotion, poor relationship with spouse or parents)? Do you want to continue to pay the cost for such an attitude? The choice is yours.

Prayer

Father, I repent of the evil of rebellion. Remind me each day that all authority is from You, and when I resist it, I am resisting You. Empower me to submit. In the name of Jesus, I pray. Amen.

Day 28

Choose to Focus on the Needs of Others

"You deserve a break today."

"Look out for Number One."

"What's in it for me?"

These popular expressions represent the attitude of our age. How did we get to the point where we are so focused on self-gratification, self-improvement, self-enlightenment, self-indulgence, and other areas with self at the center, while fewer and fewer are concerned with the needs and well-being of others?

Granted we were all born in sin and therefore have some inherent self-centeredness. However, we were also *taught* to be selfish. Now, who was the culprit, the *teacher* in your life? Was it the workaholic or absentee parent who set few spending or other limits on you because he or she felt guilty for not spending time with you? The indulgent parents who wanted to make sure you experienced every privilege that was denied them during their childhood? The absence of selfless role models? Or was it a post-childhood event, such as a deep emotional hurt that left you reeling, and you resolved to never love so selflessly again?

Or perhaps you are so overwhelmed with your own day-to-day survival that you have no energy left to think about anyone else's needs? The causes of selfishness are endless; however, they do not justify our being the central focus of our life. God expects each of his children to deny themselves and to devote their lives to unselfish service to others.

Consider a man I'll call Roy. Though he claims to be a child of God, he is one of the most selfish people I have ever met. Practically every activity in which he engages is for his own benefit. He's always thinking of how much mileage he can squeeze out of any rare act of kindness; stacking up favors that he can call in later when he needs something. Deny himself? Never!

Who enabled him to become so selfish? A host of well-meaning siblings who decided that he was special because he was the youngest of the brood—coupled with a few desperate girlfriends who couldn't resist his charm. Ask him to sacrifice a minute of his time, even for his elderly mother, and he will give you a list of excuses a mile long. His selfishness is entrenched. Oddly enough, he always has a pressing need. Selfishness keeps you trapped in lack; nothing comes into a closed hand.

Selfishness dies hard, but it is a stronghold that we must break to experience the peace and joy that give life meaning. We're going to need a lot of support to counter this negative attitude because our justifications for being the way we are will sabotage our desire to change. Here's the plan:

- Be accountable to someone and give him permission to monitor your progress.

- Look for an opportunity to share your time or talent with a worthy cause. You need to get up close and personal so that you can empathize with the plight of others.

    I had only a remote awareness of abject poverty in America until I went on a field trip to the Appalachian Mountains with World Vision USA, the Christian humanitarian organization. There I met women who told us how they had prayed for something as basic as a mop to clean their floors—right in America, the land of plenty. It broke my heart. The impact would not have been the same if I had simply read about them and sent a donation. Seeing a need firsthand nurtures your empathy and sparks a spirit of generosity.

- Give away something that you really like and would prefer to keep. (This is a good challenge for your children also.) Your goal is to begin to break your emotional attachment to stuff each day. Don't keep storing up more and more for yourself. Remember the tragic end of the rich farmer Jesus told about in His parable (see Luke 12:16-21) who did not consider sharing his overflowing harvest with others but rather boasted that he would simply build bigger barns and eat, drink, and be merry. God took his life that same day.

- Graduate to anonymous benevolence. Leave a needy person, such as a senior citizen, student, or single parent, a cash gift in an envelope. Do not put your name on it and do not tell anyone you did so. No, you can't deduct this on your income tax return, but God promises to return it so you can expect Him to do so in due season.

He who has pity on the poor lends to the LORD,
And He will pay back what he has given.
(PROVERBS 19:17)

B.C. Forbes, founder of *Forbes* magazine, said about selfishness, "I've never known any human being, high or humble, who ever regretted, when nearing life's end, having done kindly deeds. But I have known more than one millionaire who became haunted by the realization that they had led selfish lives."[8]

Let me caution that this call to selflessness is not a call to abandon your self-care. You must be on guard against sacrificing for others to the point where you not only jeopardize your health and mental well-being, but become resentful for doing so. This is not God's best. Saying no may occasionally be the appropriate response to a request. The important thing is to make the decision out of a pure heart of love and wisdom.

Prayer

Father, I thank You for every resource and advantage that You have given me. Help me to always remember that these blessings are from You and are to be shared with others for Your glory and not to be used totally for myself. In the name of Jesus, I pray. Amen.

Day 29

Choose to Pursue Excellence

The housekeeper slid the dust cloth around the edges of the stack of books on the table; however, she failed to pick up the stack and clean away the dirt underneath. *That'll do,* she thought, and she went on to the next task.

Later that evening, when the owner sat down to read, he accidentally upset the stack of books, and they all tumbled to the floor. As he began to restack them, he noticed the outline of the undusted area. "Good help is hard to find," he sighed with resignation.

Mediocrity had struck again. It has become the norm in our society.

As I write this, the anesthesia from my outpatient surgery earlier today has pretty much worn off. The hospital where the procedure was performed is under new management. When I entered the building this morning, I noticed several posted signs that implied excellence is the new order of the day. The attitudes of the sign-in security guard, the X-ray technicians, the nurses, the anesthesiologist who answered my endless questions, and everyone else I encountered demonstrated their quest for excellence and patient satisfaction. What a contrast to some of my prior experiences with certain other medical facilities.

Do you have a mediocre mindset regarding certain tasks? If so, consider the level of frustration you would experience if the people who served you had a "that'll do" attitude. What if your restaurant server delivered your food only partially cooked and your drink in a not-so-clean glass? Or what if your administrative assistant made a couple of comma corrections manually rather than keying in the corrections and reprinting the letter?

Notice how easy it is to get the picture when you think about other people's behavior?

Now hold up the mirror to your own actions. Are there any activities, assignments, or duties that you have approached with a "that'll do" mindset in your personal or professional life? For instance, are you thorough in researching a solution to a problem even if the answer lies outside your department or you may not receive credit or recognition for the results?

If you are ready to confront your mediocre attitude, the strategies below will get you onto your path to overcoming it.

Acknowledge specific areas where you have not been a model of excellence. Pray for God's intervention in your thinking so that you can begin to establish new norms in your life.

Pursue excellence rather than perfectionism. Perfectionism is just the need to be blameless. When you try to pass it off as a badge of excellence, you will find that the glory goes to you and your efforts and not to God. So avoid it. Excellence is about putting forth your very best to achieve your goal.

Realize that excellence takes time and extra effort. In fact, the "excel" in *excellence* implies that you must go beyond the norm.

I once hired an accountant who had such a mediocre attitude, I dreaded reviewing her bank reconciliations. She would allow outstanding checks and even the company's own deposits to remain in uncleared status for months without investigation. Also, when I taught accounting at a major university, I noticed some students learned only the mechanics of solving a problem but did not take the time to understand the theory behind the solution. They put themselves at a sore disadvantage.

I admit that I have a tendency to be mediocre about certain household chores. When rearranging pictures on the wall in our home, I usually hang the new picture right over the dust of the old one with the intention of cleaning it later. My husband, "Mr. Neat-so," insists on thoroughly cleaning the wall as well as the glass on the photo before hanging it—an often time-consuming undertaking. My goal, of course, like most people with a mediocre mindset toward an endeavor, is just to get done with the project and move on to the next thing.

Avoid people with poor work habits or who pooh-pooh

your efforts to be excellent. Are they achieving the kinds of results you desire?

I've worked in several environments where the chief executive traveled extensively or was rarely in the office. The old adage "when the cat is away, the mice will play" was never more true. Invariably a coworker would give me a lecture about how "corporations are not loyal anymore," "life is too short to work so hard," "the weather is too great to be stuck inside," and a litany of other excuses to justify his mediocrity. I just kept right on working.

I have also had to be on guard in my personal life, especially as a married woman. I've had single friends or people who have given up on finding a lifetime partner scoff at my efforts to maintain the fire in my marriage. "You've snared him now, why are you doing all that?" I ignore such comments. With 30 years of marriage under our belts, Darnell and I still run for the mouthwash when we hear the other pull into the garage; we value a fresh kiss. He always opens my car door, sometimes in spite of my protests when it's raining or too cold and we're scurrying to get in the car. We have cultivated the habit of going the extra mile to support each other's efforts.

Aristotle said, "We are what we repeatedly do. Excellence, then, is not an act, but a habit."

Study or observe the lives of people who have excelled in their field. Learn and model their habits. You can start right now. Think of someone whose excellence you admire. Identify one of his character traits or habits you'd like to emulate (e.g., staying focused or persevering in the face of opposition). Understand how God rewards excellence:

> *Do you see any truly competent workers?*
> *They will serve kings*
> *rather than working for ordinary people.*
> (PROVERBS 22:29 NLT)

Don't tolerate mediocrity from people under your authority. This does not mean that you become a tyrant; rather, you set and model high standards. You must also have the courage to enforce appropriate consequences when those you lead fail to adhere to those standards. Results: increased self-esteem and greater respect from others.

Perform every assignment or endeavor as if God requested it and will be evaluating your performance. Out of sight, out of mind does not apply to God; He is mindful of your every activity. "Whatever you do, work heartily, as for the Lord and not for men, knowing that from the Lord you will receive the inheritance as your reward. You are serving the Lord Christ" (Colossians 3:23-24 ESV). This alone is the best reason to maintain your strong work ethic even when the boss is not around.

Prayer

"O LORD, our Lord, how excellent is Your name in all the earth" (Psalms 8:1). I call upon You to give me the desire to be excellent in all my endeavors. Help me to live with the constant awareness of Your evaluating and loving eye so that I may do everything as unto You and not unto man. In the name of Jesus, I pray. Amen.

Day 30

Choose to Relinquish Control

Rare is the person who will readily admit to having a controlling attitude. We all know it's a toxic mindset and would prefer to give this behavior a more socially acceptable label, such as perfectionism, determination, or strong personality. Rather than force a confession from you, I'm going to ask you to take a quick quiz. Simply "tell the truth and shame the devil" (as my elders used to say), and you'll be on the road to healing in no time.

1. Do you become moody or irritated when people don't do what you want them to do?

2. Do you blame others when your mistakes are pointed out?

3. Do you generally cause stress for other people by forcing them to comply with your perfectionism or to work faster or longer?

4. Have you ever pretended to be emotionally

distressed, sick, or suicidal in order to manipulate someone's decision or to gain his attention or sympathy?

5. Do you criticize the opinions or choices of
others and thereby position yourself as superior?

6. Do you become perturbed or even abusive
(verbally or physically) when someone dis-
agrees with you or challenges your authority?

7. Are you reluctant to compliment others and
instead find yourself "fixing" something
"wrong" with them?

8. Would you find it hard to say to someone, "I
need you"?

9. Do you try to cause trouble or create distance between your spouse, friend, relative,
or coworker and someone who loves or supports them?

10. Do you bark commands at employees, waiters,
friends, your spouse, or others and omit social
niceties such as "please" and "thank you"?

While I'm no psychologist and this is not a scientific
test, I think you can render your own verdict about your
behavior. Even if you answered yes to only a couple of
these questions, you are probably battling a controlling

attitude. Have you ever stopped to consider how your behavior is affecting others? If not, let me give you a glimpse. Here is an excerpt of an email I received just today from a woman who had reached the end of her rope with her controlling friend:

> My friend and I stayed at a motel for an out-of-town Bible conference. We were assigned a non-smoking room; however, she smoked anyway. She is very forceful and controlling. I should have spoken up, but I didn't. The motel fined me $150. Further, during the weekend, my friend told me how and when to do just about everything. I held my tongue because I did not want to argue with her. Whenever I try to express my disagreements with her, she gets very upset. I seem to have a hard time drawing a line here. Help!

As I reread the email, key words jumped out: "she is very forceful"; "I seem to have a hard time drawing a line here." Little did the writer know she had revealed the solution to her problem, for herein is the secret to the controller's success: people are afraid to draw the line with them, to set and enforce relational boundaries. Therefore, like a bulldozer, controllers by the sheer force of their personality or the power of their position steamroll right over people who find it easier to submit to their domination and manipulation rather than face their wrath.

Ironically, people who are controlling are scared stiff of losing control. Relationship expert Joshua Uebergang explains,

To them, it's easier to go the route of controlling people instead of dealing with people from a level of self-respect and dignity. To them, having a controlling attitude saves energy and time. These people have visions of acting like an all-powerful God with an overruling dominance over the lives of others. Life to them is no sweat when giving the commands rather than receiving them.[9]

Jezebel, the wicked wife of Ahab king of Israel, was the consummate controller. As we saw in chapter 24, "Choose to Be Amiable," Ahab wanted to purchase a vineyard adjacent to the palace so that he could have a vegetable garden. However, Naboth, the landowner, refused to sell it to him. When Ahab related the story to Jezebel, she showed total disregard for Naboth's decision. She devised a plot to falsely accuse Naboth of wrongdoing and to have him stoned to death.

> *Then Jezebel his wife said to him, "You now exercise authority over Israel! Arise, eat food, and let your heart be cheerful; I will give you the vineyard of Naboth the Jezreelite."*
>
> *And she wrote letters in Ahab's name, sealed them with his seal, and sent the letters to the elders and the nobles who were dwelling in the city with Naboth. She wrote in the letters, saying,*
>
>> *Proclaim a fast, and seat Naboth with high honor among the people; and seat two men, scoundrels, before him to bear witness against him, saying, You have blasphemed God and*

the king. Then take him out, and stone him, that he may die.

So the men of his city, the elders and nobles who were inhabitants of his city, did as Jezebel had sent to them...

And it came to pass, when Jezebel heard that Naboth had been stoned and was dead, that Jezebel said to Ahab, "Arise, take possession of the vineyard of Naboth the Jezreelite, which he refused to give you for money; for Naboth is not alive, but dead" (1 Kings 21:7-11,15).

Okay, Ms./Mr. Controller, time to take action. Think of one person or group that you are currently controlling. What do you fear would happen if you treated them with respect by honoring their choices? Is fear and intimidation the only way that you see of holding on to the relationship? Wouldn't you rather earn their genuine love by being caring rather than callous, or are you willing to settle for "fearful submission"? Why not consider going to counseling to get to the root of the deeper issues that may be driving your behavior? For the next week, try not to criticize or rob anyone of his right to choose. Remember that even God gives people the power of choice. Continue this challenge for another two weeks or as long as it takes to get your controlling attitude under control.

I cannot conclude this chapter without admonishing you if you are a controller's victim to distance yourself from him now to protect your self-esteem and your emotional well-being. He considers your continued acquiescence as acceptance of his behavior. If the controller is your spouse, seek God's guidance for the courage to set guidelines and healthy boundaries—with consequences—for your future interactions.

Prayer

Father, I now lay this toxic attitude on Your altar. Deliver me from the fears that cause me to control others. Help me to love people the way You love them. I can't do this without Your enabling power. In the name of Jesus, I pray. Amen.

Epilogue

Your Attitude, Your Choice

To say "attitude is everything" sounds trite. But I suppose you could say that about any life-changing enduring truth—even "God loves you." The fact that it is familiar doesn't diminish its reality or its relevance.

Dr. Viktor Frankl, Austrian psychiatrist and Nazi concentration camp survivor, is my attitude hero. In relating the horrors of captivity, he explained,

> If a prisoner felt that he could no longer endure the realities of camp life, he found a way out in his mental life—an invaluable opportunity to dwell in the spiritual domain, the one that the Schutzstaffel [SS] was unable to destroy. Spiritual life strengthened the prisoner, helped him adapt, and thereby improved his chances of survival.[10]

Even if you're not physically, financially, or emotionally prepared, a strong faith keeps you fortified for the inevitable problems, frustrations, and disappointments of life.

The most effective way to maintain a great attitude is

to maintain a divine perspective on your life. You must choose to frame every negative experience in the light of God's Word. Constantly monitor yourself. If there is no reference for your specific situations, Romans 8:28 is a good catchall for every negative event: "And we know that all things work together for good to those who love God, to those who are the called according to His purpose."

I repeat this countless times each day—even yesterday when I was rushing through my garage and ripped my favorite outfit (I mean my *favorite*) on a protruding piece of metal. My first inclination was to be angry—with my husband who had been waiting (slightly impatiently) in the car and with God who allowed it to happen. I decided to practice what I've preached in the preceding chapters.

Okay, I said to myself as I took a deep breath. *I'm not going to attach any negative emotion to this situation for a few minutes. I'm just going to absorb the reality and finality of the event. The outfit is irreparably damaged. Any negative attitude I take is not going to change this. At least I didn't cut my leg. Besides, who knows what mishap this delay might be protecting us from?*

I was amazed at how I felt inside. No blaming my husband, no bemoaning the loss of the outfit. By the time I decided I wanted to deal with whatever disappointment and frustration I should have felt, the impact had been greatly minimized. I thought, *This really works!*

Do not tolerate a wrong attitude in any area of your life. From a sense of entitlement to racism or any of the 30 attitudes we have discussed, always ask yourself, *How did I develop this mindset, how is it affecting my life and relationships, and what does God say about it in His Word?* You must also be careful not to solidify a negative disposition with your words. Affirm your faith rather than your fears. Rather than saying, "This will never happen for me; I can't achieve my goal," try saying "Because I'm in right standing with God, I am surrounded with favor like a shield" (see Psalm 5:12).

Keep expecting the best from everybody, but don't get bent out of shape when people don't meet your expectations. Release them. Nobody is perfect. Just be grateful for the people that bring you joy. Endeavor to be counted among the thousands in the world with hearts of gold who serve others unselfishly every day. You will rarely find their pictures on the front pages of popular publications, but they exist.

When you have determined to exhibit a great attitude in every circumstance, you will encounter the people who need to see a "real deal" example in action. Remember this when you are tempted to retaliate, judge, or to become impatient. Say to yourself, *This is an opportunity to model a great attitude for the glory of God.*

Popular pastor and radio teacher Charles R. Swindoll sums up the essence of the message of this book. I leave you with his words:

> I believe the single most significant decision I can make on a day-to-day basis is my choice of attitude. It is more important than my past, my education, my bankroll, my successes or failures, fame or pain, what other people think of me or say about me, my

circumstances, or my position. Attitude is that "single string" that keeps me going or cripples my progress. It alone fuels my fire or assaults my hope. When my attitudes are right, there's no barrier too high, no valley too deep, no dream too extreme, no challenge too great for me.[11]

Endnotes

1. Caroline Leaf, *Who Switched Off My Brain?* (Dallas, TX: Switch on Your Brain USA Inc., 2008), 20.

2. Richard Stearns, *The Hole in Our Gospel* (Nashville: Thomas Nelson Publishers, 2009), 9.

3. Crown Financial Ministries, "Being Excellent in a Mediocre World," www.crown.org/Library/ViewArticle.aspx?ArticleId=257 (accessed March 30, 2009).

4. Deborah Smith Pegues, *30 Days to Taming Your Stress* (Eugene, OR: Harvest House Publishers, 2007), 24.

5. http://creatingminds.org/quotes/change.htm (accessed April 13, 2009).

6. http://www.anecdotage.com/browse.php?term=Sarcasm (accessed April 16, 2009).

7. Stephen R. Covey, *The Seven Habits of Highly Effective People* (New York: Simon and Schuster, 1989), 219.

8. http://www.brainyquote.com/quotes/authors/b/b_c_forbes.html (accessed April 17, 2009).

9. Joshua Uebergang, "Dealing with Controlling People," www.free-relationship-advice.org/2007/dealing-with-controlling-people.php (accessed April 7, 2009).

10. Viktor E. Frankl, *Man's Search for Meaning* (New York: Washington Square Press, 1997), 123.

11. Charles R. Swindoll, *Strengthening Your Grip* (Waco, TX: Word Books, 1982), 207.

Appendix 1
Famous Attitude Quotes

"Everything can be taken away from a man but one thing: the last of the human freedoms—to choose one's attitude in any given set of circumstances."—Viktor Frankl

"The pessimist is one who makes difficulties of his opportunities and an optimist is one who makes opportunities of his difficulties."—Harry S. Truman

"Attitude is a little thing that makes a big difference."
—Winston Churchill

"Of all the attitudes we can acquire, surely the attitude of gratitude is the most important and by far the most life-changing."—Zig Ziglar

"If I believe I cannot do something, it makes me incapable of doing it. But when I believe I can, then I acquire the ability to do it, even if I did not have the ability in the beginning."
—Mahatma Gandhi

"Attitudes are nothing more than habits of thoughts, and habits can be acquired. An action repeated becomes an attitude realized."—Paul Meier

"Do what you do so well that when other people see what it is that you do, they will want to see you do it again…and they will bring others with them to show them what it is that you do."—Walt Disney

"A happy person is not a person in a certain set of circumstances, but rather a person with a certain set of attitudes."
—Hugh Downs

"Things turn out best for the people who make the best out of the way things turn out."—Art Linkletter

"A cloudy day is no match for a sunny disposition."
—William Arthur Ward

"A loving person lives in a loving world. A hostile person lives in a hostile world; everyone you meet is your mirror."
—Ken Keyes Jr.

"A healthy attitude is contagious but don't wait to catch it from others. Be a carrier."—Tom Stoppard

"Being in a good frame of mind helps keep one in the picture of health."—author unknown

"It isn't our position but our disposition which makes us happy."—author unknown

Appendix 2

Scriptures for Maintaining a Great Attitude

Always be joyful. Never stop praying. Be thankful in all circumstances, for this is God's will for you who belong to Christ Jesus (1 Thessalonians 5:16-18 NLT).

And we know that all things work together for good to those who love God, to those who are the called according to His purpose (Romans 8:28).

For our present troubles are small and won't last very long. Yet they produce for us a glory that vastly outweighs them and will last forever! (2 Corinthians 4:17 NLT).

And we are confident that he hears us whenever we ask for anything that pleases him. And since we know he hears us when we make our requests, we also know that he will give us what we ask for (1 John 5:14-15 NLT).

For I know the thoughts that I think toward you, says the LORD, thoughts of peace and not of evil, to give you a future and a hope (Jeremiah 29:11).

"My thoughts are nothing like your thoughts," says the LORD.
   "And my ways are far beyond anything you could
      imagine.
For just as the heavens are higher than the earth,
   so my ways are higher than your ways
   and my thoughts higher than your thoughts."
      (Isaiah 55:8-9 NLT)

Dear friends, do not be surprised at the fiery ordeal that has
come on you to test you, as though something strange were
happening to you. But rejoice inasmuch as you participate in
the sufferings of Christ, so that you may be overjoyed when
his glory is revealed (1 Peter 4:12-14 NIV).

The faithful love of the LORD never ends!
   His mercies never cease.
Great is his faithfulness;
   his mercies begin afresh each morning.
(Lamentations 3:22-23 NLT)

Who is the man who desires life,
And loves many days, that he may see good?
Keep your tongue from evil,
And your lips from speaking deceit.
Depart from evil and do good;
Seek peace and pursue it…
Many are the afflictions of the righteous,
But the LORD delivers him out of them all.
(Psalm 34:12-14,19)

How to Contact the Author

Deborah Smith Pegues is an experienced certified public accountant, a Bible teacher, a speaker, a certified behavioral consultant specializing in understanding personality temperaments, and the author of *30 Days to Taming Your Tongue, 30 Days to Taming Your Stress, 30 Days to Taming Your Finances, Supreme Confidence,* and *Socially Smart in 60 Seconds.* She and her husband, Darnell, have been married since 1979 and make their home in California.

For speaking engagements, please contact the author at:

> The Pegues Group
> P.O. Box 56382
> Los Angeles, California 90056
> (323) 293-5861
>
> or
>
> E-mail: Deborah@ConfrontingIssues.com
> www.confrontingissues.com

30 DAYS TO TAMING YOUR TONGUE
What You Say (and Don't Say) Will Improve Your Relationships

DEBORAH SMITH PEGUES

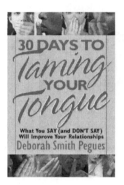

Certified behavioral consultant Deborah Pegues knows how easily a slip of the tongue can cause problems in personal and business relationships. This is why she wrote the popular *30 Days to Taming Your Tongue* (more than 700,000 copies sold). Now in trade size, Pegues' 30-day devotional will help each reader not only tame their tongue but make it productive rather than destructive.

With humor and a bit of refreshing sass, Deborah devotes chapters to learning how to overcome the

- Retaliating Tongue
- Know-It-All Tongue
- Belittling Tongue
- Hasty Tongue
- Gossiping Tongue
- 25 More!

Short stories, anecdotes, soul-searching questions, and scripturally based personal affirmations combine to make each applicable and life changing.

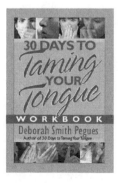

30 DAYS TO TAMING YOUR TONGUE WORKBOOK

If you're one of the thousands of readers who's found help in *30 Days to Taming Your Tongue,* this hands-on guide will help you keep on doing what you've been learning.

30 DAYS TO TAMING YOUR STRESS

Deborah Smith Pegues

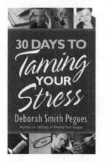

Are you sleeping well at night? Finding enough time in the day to do the things you enjoy? Sometimes stress causes us to miss out on the rest, fun, and health we long for. But you truly can tame this unruly taskmaster in 30 short days.

With insight gleaned from her experience as a behavioral consultant, Deborah Pegues will help you learn how to change self-sabotaging behavior, enjoy the present, evaluate your expectations, and release your tension.

30 DAYS TO TAMING YOUR ANGER

Deborah Smith Pegues

From Deborah Pegues comes an indispensable guide for overcoming anger and frustration. Using biblical and modern-day stories, Deborah helps you identify the destructive habits that rob you of life's fullness and derail your personal and professional relationships. You will discover anger-taming strategies such as

- extending grace to others
- conquering perfectionism
- learning to laugh at yourself

30 Days to Taming Your Anger provides Scripture-based principles, personal challenges, and faith declarations that point you to a new sense of freedom.

30 DAYS TO TAMING YOUR FEARS

Deborah Smith Pegues

Deborah Smith Pegues sheds light on rational and irrational fears and offers you a path of hope and assurance. With her trademark clarity and practical wisdom, Deborah addresses spiritual, relational, physical safety, financial, and emotional fears with godly principles and straightforward helps. Each step of the way, she gives you power over fear by helping you understand:

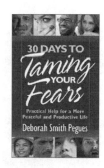

- the foundation of your fears
- God's perspective on your specific anxiety, fear, or phobia
- how to respond to fear triggers with information, awareness, and confidence
- ways to embrace healthy fears and to resist unhealthy ones
- how neutralizing your fears maximizes your life

This is an invaluable resource for anyone who is ready to exchange fear for the peace that passes all understanding.

30 DAYS TO TAMING YOUR FINANCES

Deborah Smith Pegues

Deborah Pegues gives you the benefit of her many years' experience as a public accountant and certified behavioral consultant, offering doable, practical strategies for putting your finances in order. The wealth of information you will gather includes how to

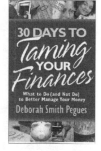

- forget past financial mistakes and start fresh
- stop emotional spending and still be content
- fund future objectives with confidence

Each day's offering will inspire and motivate you to savor the freedom that comes from organizing, valuing, and sharing your resources wisely.

CONFRONTING WITHOUT OFFENDING
Deborah Smith Pegues

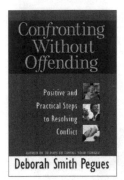

Deborah Smith Pegues shows clearly how confrontation, when done right, can be a powerful tool for mending broken relationships and for personal growth. Through her insights, you'll discover:

- whether to confront, when to confront, and which words to use
- how various personality types handle conflict
- the power of constructive criticism
- how to minimize defensiveness and hostility

Confronting Without Offending will give you the tools you need to restore peace and harmony to even the most troubled relationships at home, at work, and in any social setting.

SUPREME CONFIDENCE
Deborah Smith Pegues

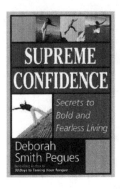

Supreme Confidence uses biblical and modern-day examples to help you recognize and overcome insecurity's many guises. Strategies such as resting in God's Word, resisting intimidation, and remembering past victories provide an effective plan of attack on self-doubt. Beyond that, you'll discover how to establish boundaries, conquer perfectionism, empower others, and embrace success.

You can understand and overcome the core fears that limit you. And you can build the confidence you need to enjoy life at home, at work, and at play!

EMERGENCY PRAYERS

Deborah Smith Pegues

We need God's help...and fast! Deborah Smith Pegues offers readers a 9-1-1 prayerbook for life's many circumstances and needs. Brief, and heartfelt, these prayers bring God's Word to the forefront of a reader's mind as they lift up cries for:

- help on the homefront
- resistance of temptations
- guidance in important decisions
- comfort in the midst of pain

SOCIALLY SMART IN 60 SECONDS

Etiquette Dos and Don'ts for Personal and Professional Success

Deborah Smith Pegues

Deborah Pegues offers 60-second etiquette solutions for awkward pauses, social situations, and everyday encounters. While other books focus on doing things right, Deborah shares how to do the right thing as she presents simple ways for readers to

- make proper and inviting introductions
- scribe personable emails, letters, and thank-you notes
- understand and be mindful of intercultural dos and don'ts
- host events, dinners, and overnight guests with ease

For everything from networking to dating to tipping, this quick and thorough guide helps readers turn their thoughts to the needs of others and practice courtesy and consideration anytime.